SPIRIT OF FLAME

To

HUGHELL FOSBROKE

FOR

G. T. S.

—

A TOKEN OF REMEMBRANCE

SPIRIT OF FLAME

A STUDY OF ST. JOHN OF THE CROSS

BY

E. ALLISON PEERS

Juan de la Cruz, espiritu de llama..
—ANTONIO MACHADO

MOREHOUSE-BARLOW CO., INC.
WILTON, CONNECTICUT 06897

NIHIL OBSTAT
John M. Fearns, S.T.D.
Censor Librorum

IMPRIMATUR

✠ *Francis Cardinal Spellman*
Archbishop, New York

New York, March 2, 1946

Foreword

THESE INTRODUCTORY PARAGRAPHS are meant for readers now meeting St. John of the Cross for the first time. Those who know him already may pass them over.

Who was he? A Spanish Carmelite friar, born just four hundred years ago, an outstanding figure of the Counter-Reformation and companion and fellow-worker to one of the greatest women the world has known, St. Teresa. As well as this, he was a writer of the first rank, both in poetry and in prose. And, most important of all, he was one of Christendom's greatest mystics.

A mystic! It sounds remote and ethereal, I know, but that is the fault of the word, which for some time past has been getting into the wrong company. Disregard the word and think only of what it means, and you will no longer be afraid of St. John of the Cross. A mystic is *a person who has fallen in love with God*. We are not afraid of lovers—no, indeed: "all the world loves a lover." They attract us by their ardour, their single-mindedness, their yearning to be one with the object of their love. It was in just that way that St. John of the Cross thought about God and strove after God, longing, too, that others should do the same.

That is the whole secret of the amazing power of his life, his character and his writings.

This is not the first attempt I have made to present St. John of the Cross to English readers. Ten years ago, in my Rede Lecture at Cambridge, I drew a picture of him, primarily for a small university circle. Three years later, I had the satisfaction of being able to publish his complete works in English, and in a single edition, for the first time. Now I am trying to introduce him to many who have neither the time nor the training to study the three large volumes of the *Works*.

Not merely to commemorate the quatercentenary of his birth, but because I believe that the world to-day has the most urgent need of lovers *a lo divino*, I have written this little book in the midst of the preoccupations of the War. Perhaps it is as well that the quatercentenary should have fallen at a time when the bankruptcy of our inadequate application of Christianity has become so evident. If in building our new world we look more closely at the rigid standards shown us by Christ we shall find that we are building upon firmer foundations than before. And those are the standards of St. John of the Cross. Rereading him as I have been in these days of crisis, when the faith of many is burning low and men's hearts are failing them for fear, I have felt more keenly than ever the contrast between the world's tone and his. More convincingly and more triumphantly he has pointed, beyond our wrecked ambitions, to the King's Highway of the Holy Cross; more vividly has one realized that that is the only way to be trodden by a civilization which has tried every other.

A few passages from this book have appeared, in substance, in the weekly Press—the *Guardian*, the *Church Times*, the *Tablet*, the *Universe* and the *British Weekly*, to the editors of which periodicals I desire to make the usual acknowledgments. The comprehensiveness of the list is one more illustration of the appeal made by the mystics to all who love our Lord Jesus Christ in sincerity: may this greatest of mystics long continue to play his part in bringing them nearer together.

E. A. P.

University of Liverpool
1942

Contents

PRINCIPAL ABBREVIATIONS

Baruzi: Jean Baruzi: *Saint Jean de la Croix et le problème de l'expérience mystique.* Paris, 1924.

P. Bruno: P. Fr. Bruno de Jésus-Marie, C.D.: *Saint John of the Cross.* London, 1932. (Reference is given to the English translation: where the original text [Paris, 1929] is referred to, this is explicitly stated.)

P. Crisógono: P. Fr. Crisógono de Jesús Sacramentado, C.D.: *San Juan de la Cruz, su obra científica y su obra literaria.* Madrid, 1929. 2 vols.

Frost: Bede Frost: *Saint John of the Cross.* London, 1937.

P. Silverio: *Obras completas de San Juan de la Cruz,* ed. P. Fr. Silverio de Santa Teresa, C.D. Burgos, 1929-31. 5 vols.

R.L.: E. Allison Peers: *Saint John of the Cross.* The Rede Lecture for 1932. Cambridge, 1932.

Studies: E. Allison Peers: *Studies of the Spanish Mystics.* London, 1927-30. 2 vols.

Works: The Complete Works of St. John of the Cross, Doctor of the Church. Translated and edited by E. Allison Peers. London, 1934-5. 3 vols.

It should be noted that where a commentary is referred to, its title is given in italics (e.g., *Living Flame of Love*); where the corresponding poem is meant, it is placed between quotation marks (e.g., "Living Flame of Love"). In Part II the titles of the commentaries as given in footnotes are abbreviated.

References to the *Letters* of St. Teresa are to P. Silverio's edition (Burgos, 1922-4). All passages translated from St. Teresa are taken from my forthcoming edition of her *Complete Works.*

PART I

THE MYSTIC IN SIXTEENTH-CENTURY SPAIN

CHAPTER I

Early Life

O**N AN UNKNOWN DAY** of the year 1542,[1] in the village of Fontiveros, some thirty miles north-west of St. Teresa's native city of Ávila, was born a child destined to become a Doctor of the Church Universal and one of the greatest Christian mystics who have ever lived.

That humble village stands on the lofty, wind-swept plateau of Castile; and it is both appropriate and stimulating to associate a Saint whose teaching, uncompromising and austere, was always so sharply outlined, and whose whole life was directed towards so clearly envisaged a goal, with the keenness and purity of that mountain climate. Beneath the incredible blue of the Castilian sky, and the unearthly stillness of that desert-like plain, one seems immeasurably nearer the things of Heaven than in crowded city streets or in the fog and cloud of a northern climate. In that diaphanous atmosphere, illumined by the most brilliant sunshine, one has the illusion of being able to see, not only to the distant

[1] Perhaps on Midsummer Day. The parish registers were destroyed by a fire four years after his birth and the only serious evidence as to the day is an inscription on the font, which is dated 1689. Midsummer Day being also the Feast of St. John Baptist, however, this attribution may well have been a pure conjecture.

horizon, but to the very end of the world. Just so, as the reader of St. John of the Cross becomes gradually transformed into the disciple, the busy present seems to fall away from him, the stillness of the desert to enfold him, the life of the Spirit to become more real, and the sun, even as it relentlessly picks out his imperfections, to clothe him with a new warmth and radiance.

From the day when I first experienced the stern but thrilling beauty of Castile, I was glad that St. John of the Cross had been born there. Now, after a quarter of a century spent in ever-increasing intimacy with his thought, it seems impossible that he could have been born anywhere else.

His family name was Juan de Yepes. On his father's side he was well descended; on his mother's, less so. The father had displeased his family by marrying out of his class; and, having as a result of this to earn his own livelihood, had learned his wife's accomplishment of weaving. At the best, their circumstances would seem to have been humble.

When Juan was about seven years of age, his father died, and soon afterwards the mother and her two sons (a third had died young) removed to Arévalo —probably their nearest town—which lies on the main road from Madrid to the north-west, and later to what in the sixteenth century was a large city, a busy centre of international trade and a royal residence, Medina del Campo. Juan's mother had taken up her weaving again and there would have been more custom for her in Medina than in a smaller town, besides more opportunity for promising children to get a good education. Young Juan, who had been sent in turn by his persevering mother to a carpenter, a tailor, a sculptor and a painter, but showed less aptitude for these trades than for study, was put to school in the College of the Children of Doctrine.

He must have done well there, for he quickly found the patron so necessary in those days to academic success. Don Antonio Álvarez de Toledo was a devout man who had retired from whatever his business may have been, in order, not to enjoy his leisure, but to take up social work as warden of a hospital. He adopted Juan, then aged about fourteen, and, in return for services of the kind a boy could render, provided for his education, with the idea that he should in due course train for Holy Orders and come back to him again as hospital chaplain.

So, between the ages of fourteen and nineteen, Juan worked in the hospital and studied at a school newly founded by the Society of Jesus, which at that time had been in existence for only about twenty years. How complete an education he gained there it is difficult to say. Documentary testimony suggests that it was limited to "grammar lessons," which would occupy hardly more than two hours daily, and no doubt his work in the hospital was exacting. If this was so, his later academic record suggests that he must have worked hard in his leisure. We know that he came under the influence of a brilliant young master called P. Bonifacio, and such influence of a master on a boy is seldom restricted to class-hours. Possibly it was some enthusiasm fanned by this young Father which lay beneath an episode narrated by his brother. "And our mother used to say that they once went to look for him at midnight and found him studying among the faggots."

It may well have been during the time spent with the Jesuits that Juan found his vocation. That he did not join the Society is quite understandable. The system of St. Ignatius, as we have it in the *Spiritual Exercises*, is, in its constant use of meditation and imagery, so unlike the type of contemplation which attracted the Carmelite Saint that one would hardly deduce any great similarity of thought between them. Evidently the ideals of the life of contemplation had made their appeal to him while he was still in his teens; for, a year after leaving the hospital, instead of becoming a Jesuit or (as his patron would have liked) deciding to train for the secular priesthood, he took the habit of the Order of Carmel.

There was a house of that Order at Medina, dedicated to St. Anne, and this he entered in 1563. It is generally asserted that he took the habit on the Feast of St. Matthias (February 24), and it is true that the new name he assumed was John of St. Matthias, but there is also ground for believing that the date was in August or September. In the following year—at some time between May and October—he was professed, and in November 1564 he entered the University of Salamanca, where he took a three-year Arts course, residing at St. Andrew's, the College of his Order in Salamanca, which was affiliated to the University.

It will not be easy for the traveller in Spain to visit all the places associated with the life of the Carmelite Saint: many of them are far from the beaten track and entirely without facilities for lodging. But Salamanca, like Ávila, is accessible, hospitable and rich in mediaeval memories. The once great University of Salamanca, now a shell of its former self, comes to life as one walks in it, and it is easy to picture the days when its lecture rooms, with their rough benches and tall hooded pulpits, were thronged with cassocked students drawn from all parts of Spain and indeed of Europe. For Salamanca was one of the four leading universities in Europe; and as Fray Luis de León, a professor there in John's time, succinctly put it, "the light of Spain and of Christendom."

Besides reading Arts at the University of Salamanca, John studied Theology at St. Andrew's:[2] his course must therefore have been a very full one, and, if he had in addition to make up any deficiencies in his earlier education, he would have needed to work at great pressure. This, however, would be no trouble to the youth who had begun his studies at dead of night among the faggots. His University and College

[2] Baruzi, p. 122; P. Crisógono, I, 25-6.

courses completed, he was ordained to the priesthood in the summer of 1567, intending, perhaps—
for there is some doubt here—to return to Salamanca, and begin a year's Theology at the University in the autumn. It must have been almost immediately after his ordination that the nature and
extent of his life's work were revealed to him.

The revelation came, not by some supernatural
manifestation, nor even in a dream so vivid that the
pious might interpret it as a Divine vision, but in
the most ordinary and practical way possible. Even
to-day, religiously minded young people are apt to
expect God to send them, not only opportunities for
discovering their life's work, but clear indications
as to whether they should reject them, defer their
acceptance or embrace them immediately. In real
life God seldom works in that way. He gives us
certain good desires, and a certain degree of ability
and intelligence, and leaves us to look out for opportunities of putting our ability to the best use and to
be guided by our intelligence as to the acceptance
or the rejection of them when they arise.

So it was with Fray John of St. Matthias. Not that
he was a stranger to visions. As a child of four or five,
he had fallen into a pond, and had believed he saw a
"beautiful lady" whom his upbringing prompted
him to suppose to be the Queen of Heaven. It was
not the beautiful apparition, however, but a con-
veniently passing workman, who had pulled him
out. A similar process took place with regard to his

vocation. One day, when he was still a youth, there came to him some words which seemed to have been spoken by God. "Thou shalt serve Me," they ran, "in an Order whose former perfection thou shalt help to restore." At the time the words were meaningless to him and he could only store them up in his memory and hope that some day they would be made plain. He was not disappointed; though the interpretation, when it came, was supplied by no supernatural visitant but by a middle-aged lady.

The lady was, of course, St. Teresa. When he first met her, in 1567, probably early in September, he was twenty-five, and she fifty-two. It is strange to reflect that for the whole of his life the two had lived only a few miles apart and yet that in all probability neither had ever heard of the other. Strange, for that matter, to us who think so little of travelling half across Europe, that John's twenty-five years should have been spent within an area forming an irregularly shaped square, the longest side of which measured barely fifty miles. But now they were both to travel up and down Spain and to remain in the closest contact until the elder died, nine years before the younger.

St. Teresa (Teresa of Jesus, to give her the name by which she was known during her lifetime) had spent nearly thirty years, from the time when she entered the Carmelite Order at the age of about eighteen down to the year in which John left his hospital, as a simple nun in the Convent of the Incarnation, at Ávila. But life at the Incarnation was easy, discipline was lax and the sisters lived almost as much in the world as out of it. So Teresa asked and obtained permission to adopt for herself the stricter and primitive Carmelite rule of life and to found a convent of her Order based upon it. There thus came into being the "Discalced," or Barefooted, Order of Carmelites, on the roll of which are so many great mystics and saints. For five years more she remained at Ávila, in this new house, dedicated to St. Joseph, after which, feeling the venture to have been been successful, she began to consider going farther afield. Profiting by a visit of the General of the Order, she asked and obtained of him a licence to found further religious houses of the Reform for women, and also, on the understanding that there should be no separation between Reform and Observance,[3] two houses for men. But now, as she tells us in her *Book of the Foundations*, came a serious obstacle. Having few acquaintances, she knew of no single friar in the Province who would collaborate with her, nor had she so much as a single house at her disposal in which the new experiment could be begun.

But she was fortunate in that the first step which she took led straight to the solution of her problem. She decided to establish the second of her convents for women at Medina del Campo. Here Fray Antonio de Heredia, whom she had known in Ávila and who

[3] Cf. P. Zimmerman, in P. Bruno, p. 363, and elsewhere.

had recently gone thence to be Prior of the very monastery in which Fray John had professed, had promised to obtain a house for her. She arrived, after a fatiguing journey, at midnight on August 14, 1567. The house, though duly found, was such a tumbledown structure that two months had to be spent on its repair. During this period Teresa and her nuns were the guests of a merchant, who allowed them to use the upper part of his own large house, where they were completely independent.[4]

She had now leisure to think out her other project —the extension of the Reform to men's houses— about which, she tells us, she was "continually preoccupied." She discussed it, "in the strictest confidence," with her friend Fray Antonio, who, much to her surprise, not only gave it his emphatic approval but offered to be the first to join. Teresa, a little disconcerted, thought at first that he was joking. Fray Antonio was a good man, studious, earnest and devout; but it had never occurred to her to think of him as a reformer, and she doubted whether either his temperament or his health would stand the austerity of her Rule. He insisted, however, that "for many days the Lord had been calling him to a stricter life, that he had already resolved to go to the Carthusians and that they had assured him that they would receive him."[5] Still Teresa was not quite happy about his resolution, so she suggested that he

[4] St. Teresa: *Foundations,* Chapter III.
[5] *Ibid.*

should practice the Primitive Rule privately for a time and see how it suited him. At the end of a year he had come out of the ordeal so well that her scruples were vanquished.

Fray Antonio's period of probation had hardly begun than Teresa found her second recruit—Fray John of St. Matthias. Exactly how they came to meet is not known. She tells us, however, that John had also been thinking of embracing a stricter Rule by joining the Carthusian Order, which had an old-established monastery not far away, at El Paular, in the heart of the barely accessible Guadarramas. It seems likely, then, that he had been in consultation with his Prior, and, hearing what had happened, had determined to go and see her ,too. So one day, "shortly afterwards"—presumably early in September 1567—she received a visit from this "young Father who was studying at Salamanca," accompanied by a fellow-student, Fray Pedro de Orozco, who seems to have been a warm admirer of Fray John, for he told her "great things" about his life and character. She took to her second recruit immediately, and was as confident about accepting him as she had been dubious about taking his Prior. So she explained to him exactly what she had in view,[6] pointed out how much more satisfactory it would be for him to remain in his own Order if it could give him what he wanted; and "begged him earnestly" to

[6] He "needed no testing, for . . . he had always led a life of great perfection and religious zeal" (St. Teresa: *Foundations*, Chapter XIII). Cf. P. Bruno, p. 57.

take no further steps about his project until she had found a house for her first friars to live in.

Whether or no John foresaw in Teresa's proposal the fulfilment of the prophecy so long in his mind we cannot say, nor do we know how near he came to joining the Order of St. Bruno. He promised her, however, to curb his youthful impatience, and, "provided there were no long delay,"[7] to wait as she had asked him. Meanwhile he went back to the University, where he devoted a further year to the study of Theology—that same year which Fray Antonio was spending in testing himself in the new Rule and Teresa in waiting for her two friars to come to her and in looking for a suitable house for them to live in.

How clearly these three figures stand out before us! Teresa, the woman of fifty-two, her face lined by ill-health and austere discipline, but her humorous, sensitive mouth and her keen, twinkling eyes testifying to her shrewdness and understanding of human nature. Fray Antonio, a man of fifty-seven, tall, finely set up, with the slight stoop of the scholar and an air of authority acquired from long exercise of it—somewhat modified, perhaps, by a certain diffidence and constraint at the position of postulant in which he now found himself. Fray John, a diminutive boyish figure of five feet two inches, with the high forehead of the intellectual, the quiet, self-possessed mien of the man of character, the far-away expression of the

[7] St. Teresa: *Foundations*, Chapter III.

visionary and the unfaltering and penetrating gaze
of the mystic. "Now I have a friar and a half to begin
the Reform with!" cried Teresa in delight when she
rejoined her companions, who were at recreation,
after that first interview. Admirers of St. John of the
Cross, from his own days onwards, have tried to
prove that by the half-friar she must have meant Fray
Antonio, referring to her doubt of his powers of
endurance. But that would hardly have been an
appropriate subject for so casual a remark; and I feel
sure that St. Teresa would in no circumstances have
joked about a man's spiritual unreadiness, especially
if she were uncertain of it, or for that matter about
his delicate health. Smallness of stature was another
matter—and she did, in fact, refer to Fray John's
lack of inches in a letter written about a year later.[8]
A man's height was a mere accident, like his financial
circumstances or his profession; spiritual deficiencies
or delicacy of health were afflictions. Yes, I think we
may safely take it that the "half-friar" was St. John
of the Cross.

Of Fray John's post-graduate course in Salamanca
we know practically nothing; we take up his history
again in May 1568, when the academic year was
over. Eager now to begin his new work, he went with
his Prior, as soon as he returned to Medina, to see
Teresa, and learned from her that a benefactor from
Ávila had provided them with a house in a village
not far from that city called Duruelo.

[8] St. Teresa: *Letters*, X (end of September 1568). The passage is
quoted on p. 17.

It was no great acquisition, one would suppose. The village comprised about twenty houses, and the benefactor's gift-house had for a long time been un-inhabited. "Although I saw what kind of place it would be," remarks Teresa in her account of the episode, resignedly, "I praised Our Lord and gave Him hearty thanks."[9]

As soon as she was able, she went, with a sister nun and a chaplain from Ávila, to see it. So concise and vivid is her own report that it can hardly be improved upon.

Although we set out early in the morning, we were unfamiliar with the road, and so we went astray; and, as little is known of the place, we could find no one to direct us. We travelled all that day in the greatest discomfort, for the sun was very strong. When we thought we were near the village, we found we had as far again still to go. I always remember the fatigue of that long, round-about journey. We arrived only a little before nightfall.

When we entered the house, we found it in such a condition that we dared not spend the night there, so dirty was it and so numerous were the harvesters who were about. It had a fair-sized porch, a room divided into to, with a loft above it, and a little kitchen; that is all there was of the building which was to be our monastery.

I thought that the porch might be made into a church, that the loft would do quite well for the choir and that the friars could sleep in the room below. But my companion, though a much better person than I am and a

[9] St. Teresa: *Foundations*, Chapter XIII.

great lover of penance, could not bear the thought of my founding a monastery there. "Mother," she said, "I am certain that nobody, however good and spiritual, could endure this. You must not consider it."[10]

These were the conditions which Teresa reported to the Prior when she reached Medina again. Could he possibly put up with them, she asked him? If he could, it would be well worth while for him to go there. First and foremost, if he accepted what God had given them, He would undoubtedly soon smooth their paths. Secondly, if they proposed beginning their work in a pretentious house they would never obtain leave from the Provincials, and the General had made his own leave conditional upon this. Fray Antonio's reply exceeded Teresa's highest hopes. Of course he would go and live in such a place as she had described; if it were necessary, he would live in a pigsty.

That settled the matter. Fray Antonio might be frail in health, but he was a man of mature years and he had made a considered decision. So, before he resigned his office at Medina, Teresa suggested his occupying himself with the provision of some necessaries for the new house, while Fray John went with her for a short time to Valladolid. Here, during the time he had been away at Salamanca, she had founded another convent, and she was anxious that he should see something of life under the new Rule and absorb as much as he could of its spirit. The

[10] *Ibid.*

Valladolid nuns had not completely settled in their house, for the workmen were still engaged in making it habitable. But, under Teresa's guidance, he was able to appreciate the nature and purpose of the severity of their *régime*, and also to gain some idea of how they got on together, which was best done during the daily hours of recreation. This was the first time that Teresa had had her young recruit to herself for any continuous period. He impressed her tremendously. "He was so good a man that I, at least, could have learned much more from him than he from me," she recorded later in her *Foundations*.[11] And, when he left Valladolid for his new home, she gave him a long letter of introduction to Don Francisco de Salcedo, a gentleman living in Ávila, where he would have to stay on his way to Duruelo. A few sentences from this letter have become classical:

I beg your Honour to have a talk with this Father and help him in this matter, for, though small in stature, I know he is great in God's eyes. We shall certainly miss him sorely here, for he is prudent and well-fitted for our way of life, to which I believe Our Lord has called him. There is not a friar but speaks well of him, for his life [in the Order], though short, has been one of great penitence. The Lord seems to be leading him by the hand. We have had some differences here about business matters; I myself have been at fault and have sometimes been vexed with him, but we have never seen the least imperfection in him."[12]

[11] *Ibid.*
[12] St. Teresa: *Letters*, X (end of September 1568).

That was the impression which the younger of the two saints, upon their first close contact, made on the elder. That was the John of St. Matthias, henceforward to be John of the Cross, who went southward from Valladolid to meet his first trials at Duruelo.

CHAPTER II

From Duruelo To Ávila

ONCE THE APPROVAL of the Provincials was obtained, there was little further need of preparation. At the end of September, John, being the younger and freer of the two, went on to Duruelo to put the house in order, accompanied, from Ávila onward, by a workman to do the heavy labour, while Antonio first came to see Teresa at Valladolid to tell her of the preparations he had made, and then, after formally resigning his office of Prior went south to join his young companion.

Antonio—now to be Antonio of Jesus—seems to have been a somewhat slow, meticulous person, if we may judge from the little he did during the weeks of preparation just referred to and the fact that John had already been at Duruelo for two months when at length he arrived. On his coming to report progress to Teresa, "the only article with which he was well provided was clocks, of which he had five."[1] Teresa was vastly amused, but Antonio, who was probably seldom amused about anything, retorted that he was certainly not going to Duruelo without provision for keeping regular hours. But he was full of the spirit of the Reform—the spirit of complete detachment.

[1] St. Teresa: *Foundations*, Chapter XIV.

When he came in sight of the village, he told her later, he felt a very great inward happiness. At last, after spending so many years as a friar, he was about to leave the world in a truer sense than he had ever done before and plunge into a Divine solitude.[2]

Of John's feelings there is no record, but all his work is so deeply impregnated with the spirit of detachment that we may be sure he welcomed the two months of poverty and solitude in which he could learn to know that world which he outlines for us in his terse and penetrating maxims:

Love consists not in feeling great things, but in having great detachment and in suffering for the Beloved.

Whatever thought of ours is not centered upon God is stolen from Him.

The solitary bird . . . can endure no companionship, even of its own kind.

Divest thyself of what is human in order to seek God.

Walk in solitude with God.

Live in this world as though there were in it but God and thy soul, so that thy heart may be detained by naught that is human.[3]

Freed at last from the intercourse of both lecture-room and cloister, he had at Duruelo the opportunity of testing his vocation in the fullest degree—an opportunity which both at Medina and at Salamanca had been denied him.

It was on the eve of Advent Sunday, November 27, 1568, that Fray Antonio, with a companion, "a

[2] *Ibid.*

[3] "Points of Love," 36, 37, 42, 54, 57, 61 (*Works*, III, 253-6).

young man not in orders,"[4] who, under the name
Joseph of Christ, was to make the third friar of the
Reform, arrived at Duruelo. On the following morning the first Community Mass was said and the three
friars took their fresh vows. The new names they had
assumed, it will be observed, as a symbol of their
resolve to lead completely new lives, were those of
Jesus, Christ and the Cross: they were determined
to know nothing save Jesus Christ and Him Crucified.

Their excessively austere and simple but supremely happy life varied little. A large part of each
day and night they devoted to the recital of the choir
offices, to devotional reading and study, to the celebration of Mass, and to solitary converse with God
such as they had learned to practise from the earthly
life of Christ Himself. They had food to obtain and
to prepare;[5] and at first they may have thought of
growing some of this themselves, for, though on the
Castilian plateau winter is severe and spring comes
late, their house was situated amid green fields, not
far from a river. But, as they gradually became
known about the countryside, this proved unnecessary. "Of food they had quite enough," recounts St.

[4] St. Teresa: *Foundations*, Chapter XIV.

[5] Baruzi (p. 73, n. 4) quotes evidence from a manuscript source
that John's mother, brother and sister-in-law kept house for the
community. But this, I think, for obvious reasons, can only have
been for some short period, though P. Bruno (p. 88) evidently takes
it as having lasted for a long time. P. Silverio (I, 53-4) quotes an
early account of one of John's mission visits in which he is said to
have been accompanied by his brother.

Teresa, "for the villages in the district would provide them with more than they needed."[6]

A considerable part of their time they employed in evangelizing the surrounding country. As the houses were scattered and there was no town or even large village within several miles' radius, their sphere of action, though limited in extent, was clearly marked out for them. They would leave the friary each morning, soon after Mass, walk out, now in one direction, now in another, for six, eight or ten miles, preach, visit, hear confessions and return home for their evening meal "very late." Some years afterwards it was laid down that friars of the Reform should wear the hemp-soled sandals known as *alpargatas*. But these pioneers interpreted their Rule quite literally, and walked everywhere, even through the deep snow, barefoot. Yet *con el contento todo se les hacía poco*: "this was very little trouble to them, so happy were they."

Some three months after their arrival, they received their first visit from the Mother Foundress. A characteristically vivid picture of their friary, which she penned about four years later, shows how striking was the impression it had left on her. The "little Bethlehem of a porch," as she called it, had been turned into the humblest church that had ever existed. There was room at the altar only for the priest; the "congregation" had to enter the house and climb up to the loft, which served as the choir. So low was

[6] St. Teresa: *Foundations*, Chapter XIV.

the loft that even the little "half-friar" had to stoop
to enter it; so they said the choir offices in the centre,
where alone, apparently, they could stand upright.[7]

When Teresa had first seen the "little house," her
idea had probably been that each of the two friars
should live and sleep in one of the two divisions of
its only living-room. But since then their numbers
had grown to three, and soon the three were joined
by a friar belonging to the original Rule, who was
too infirm to take the vows of the Reform but
wished for a time to share their fellowship. So the
living-room was turned over to this Father and Fray
Joseph and at each corner of the loft was made a
"little hermitage"—possibly wooden partitions were
run up by the workman whom John had brought
with him. This provided John and Antonio with
accommodation, about as devoid of comfort as it is
possible to imagine. Its only furniture, apart from
two stones which served the friars as pillows, con-
sisted of bundles of hay ("as the place was very cold,"
explains Teresa, apologetically); and the sloping roof
was so low that it "almost came down on their
heads," so that they could only sit or lie. In each of
these cells there was an opening in the outer wall,
which served as a window, from which its occupant
could see the altar below. For a great part of the
bitter winter nights the friars would remain in their
wind-swept loft, first saying Matins, then remaining
absorbed in private prayer till it was time to say

[7] *Ibid.*

Prime. And sometimes, on rising from their devotions, they would find that, without their having observed it, their habits had become covered with snow.[8]

This was surely the extreme limit of the simple life. The worldly might even describe it as sub-human. St. Teresa tells us that two business men who accompanied her in that first spring when she visited Duruelo on her way to Toledo found the little friary depressing in the extreme, though afterwards they assured her that they would not have missed coming for the world. Not only did the unfurnished loft, the living-room and the kitchen-refectory seem to them inadequate accommodation for four grown men, but there was something rather gruesome in the only adornments which the place permitted itself. "There were so many crosses about," comments St. Teresa, "and so many skulls!" The skulls, of course, served to remind the friars of the shortness of their life on earth; the crosses, of the sufferings of their Redeemer. But she, regarding it all with the insight of love, had no emotion but one of amazement that the Lord should have inspired such spirituality. She recalled, in particular, a little cross which she had noticed in the church, above the vessel containing the holy water. It was made of plain wood: the friars had no money for buying crucifixes. But they had fastened to it a paper picture of Christ—"and it seemed to inspire greater devo-

[8] *Ibid.*

tion," she exclaims, "than if it had been a crucifix of the finest workmanship." But the sight that made her happiest of all was her first view of the friary as she approached it on that Lenten morning. There, in front of her, sweeping out the porch, was the tall and dignified ex-Prior of Medina.

"How is this, Father!" exclaimed Teresa, always full of fun. "Whatever has become of your reputation?"

And Antonio, so she relates, merely looked up, "with that happy expression which never leaves him."

"I curse the time," he replied, "when I ever had any."[9]

So extreme was the friars' austerity—stopping short, it would seem, at no kind of corporal penance —that before leaving them Teresa, fearful lest it should frighten off recruits, remonstrated with them about it—quite unsuccessfully, and also, as it proved, quite needlessly. They quickly won both followers and admirers.

The fact is that genuine spirituality invariably inspires respect, and, though many religious reformers have at first had to endure the uncomprehending world's enmity and persecution, they have always ended by asserting their influence upon it. St. John of the Cross, in due course, was to be allotted his full share of persecution, but at this stage he and his companions were welcomed wherever they went.

[9] *Ibid.*

Spain is pre-eminently a country of devout lay-folk; and even at times when the forces of atheism have been rampant, men and women who in the religious life have vowed themselves to the service of God and their neighbour have been loved and reverenced by the masses as they deserve. Not only were the friars given food by the peasants in return for their ministrations, but their congregations were swelled by the well-to-do, who would actually journey to the modest friary to make their confessions. And having seen with their own eyes how poor it was, they may have begun, like Teresa's business friends, to feel depressed—possibly, too, a little uncomfortable, if they had any unoccupied houses of their own.[10]

So before long the friars began to receive offers of houses and building sites, one of which at length they felt bound to accept. A certain Don Luis de Toledo, a local aristocrat who was known as "Lord of the Five Towns," had inherited from his parents a magnificent picture of Our Lady, originally acquired by his father in Flanders. So greatly did he prize it that in a village called Mancera, where he was the principal landowner, he had erected a church as a worthy setting for it: St. Teresa describes it as a *retablo*, so he had probably had it made into an altar-piece. Hearing of the Discalced Friars, he asked Fray Antonio, whom the Provincial had appointed Prior of their little community, to come and see him, showed him the picture and offered to erect

[10] *Ibid.*

them a friary near the church, if they would move there.

The house was built, Fray Antonio sharing in the manual labour, and on St. Barnabas' Day (June 11) 1570, after living for rather more than eighteen months at Duruelo, the three friars of the Reform, with some others—perhaps as many as fourteen[11]— who had subsequently joined them, established themselves at Mancera. The ceremony of the inauguration of the new house marked a great advance in solemnity upon that simple Advent morning service in the porch of the house at Duruelo. The friars were well known all around, and the country people "could not say enough about their sanctity and the great good they were doing in the villages."[12] So the church was thronged with peasantry, and in the sanctuary were the Carmelite Provincial and a number of friars of the Observance. Soon after the inauguration, the community was increased by the profession of two more friars.

This new house of the Reform was "exceedingly magnificial" by comparison with the "little house" of Duruelo. It lacked only a water supply, and this was provided in a way which, according to St. Teresa, was "considered miraculous." The fact seems to be that Fray Antonio possessed the powers of a water-diviner: at any rate he went into the cloisters one evening with a stick in his hand, stopped at a certain

[11] Cf. P. Silverio, I, 57.
[12] St. Teresa: *Foundations*, Chapter XIV.

point, made a peculiar motion with the stick, and said, "Now, dig here." And, reports St. Teresa, "they had dug only a very little way when so much water gushed out that it is difficult now to stop it."[13]

Down to this point the personality of the little sub-prior and novice-master (for it was with these titles that John was dignified at Duruelo) has been overshadowed by that of the older and more experienced Fray Antonio, and the narratives which guide us subordinate his own doings to those of the community as a whole. Antonio, though he lived to a venerable old age and in fact survived his junior, now fades out of the story, but John, too, does little of note between his twenty-eighth year, in which he went to Mancera, and his thirty-fifth, in which he suddenly emerges in a picture of the utmost clarity. During the intervening period, he was growing steadily in maturity, spirituality and learning. So, marked though it is by a great deal of superficial activity, it must be thought of as a period of inward preparation and growth.

For three of these years, during which recruits in some numbers began to join the infant Reform, he held the office of novice-master, first at Mancera, and, from October 1570, at Pastrana, where Fray Antonio had inaugurated the second Reformed foundation for men, with four professed friars and ten novices, on July 13, 1569. Mancera and Pastrana made up the

[13] *Ibid.*

two foundations of the Reform for which alone Teresa had received a licence; but while permission was being sought to found more, a Discalced College, something like the St. Andrew's which John had attended at Salamanca, was established in connection with Spain's brand-new—"modern"—university at Alcalá de Henares. Obviously the man to be put in charge of such a college was this young graduate of Salamanca, already known among his contemporaries as a scholar. It was in the spring of 1571 that he went there, and he stayed for a little over a year, acting at the same time as spiritual director to the Carmelite nuns in the city. In April 1572 he was recalled for a few weeks to Pastrana, to help his successor, whom the novices had found excessively severe. In the summer we hear of his being once more in his home country. At some time between May and September, he and Fray Germán of St. Matthias, another Pastrana friar, were sent as confessors to Teresa's original convent of the Incarnation, at Ávila. Living with his colleague in a little house near the convent, he remained there, in undisturbed seclusion, for fully five years, until the beginning of the terrible trials from which sprang the great gifts which he was to bestow upon posterity.

Of his appointment to the Incarnation the most interesting feature is that, during about half the time of John's stay at Ávila, Teresa herself was there. She had been ordered back to her own convent as Prioress, in July 1571, and went there in October. At the time she was in the middle of a busy existence as foundress of Discalced houses, but the Reform was still subject to the rules and discipline of the Observance and she had no choice but to obey. The Incarnation, it appears, had been getting laxer and laxer since the years when she had referred to it, none too favourably even then, in the *Book of Her Life*, and the task before her was to infuse into it some of her own spirit.

In this, as her extant letters testify, she appears to have succeeded, though at the cost of great spiritual suffering. It was hard to go back from the keen, invigorating atmosphere of discipline, detachment and effort which she had created to the enervating air in which she had been brought up. The reception given her was not a reassuring one, and she found no sympathetic director to whom she could open her griefs. That winter of 1571 must also have been a winter for her soul. But after winter comes summer, and with the summer of 1572 came her beloved "little friar," John of the Cross.

Few details have been recorded of John's experiences in Ávila, but conjecture and imagination have here a wonderful field of opportunity. How, we wonder, did this large community of one hundred and thirty nuns—good, bad and indifferent—react to the inflexible standards prescribed for them by the austere young Discalced friar? That his advent had a salutary effect on them we know from Teresa herself. He can only have been there a very short

time when she told her sister what "great good is
being done by this Discalced Father who is hearing
confessions here, Fray John of the Cross."[14] Less than
five months later she was describing to a former confessor what a complete change had come over the
house since the summer. There was no more trouble
there now about obedience or recollection than in
her own Discalced convent, St. Joseph's. A month
previously the Visitor had been quite unable to find
any cause for complaint. "The Lord seems to be
granting so much grace to these souls all at once that
I am astonished at it."[15] And this improvement she
attributes largely to the new confessor: "he has done
a great deal of good."[16]

Still more interesting is it to picture the relations
of growing intimacy which developed between *el
Santo* and *la Santa,* as present-day Carmelites call
them. After all, the two founders had so far seen
comparatively little of each other. Those brief talks
at Medina, those few weeks at Valladolid, that flying
visit to Duruelo—there was hardly a chance here for
either to exert any permanent influence upon the
other. John, still so young, must have learned much
from Teresa's experience; Teresa, who writes so
often and with such respect of *letrados,*[17] and so wist-
fully of the rarity with which erudition in a director

[14] St. Teresa: *Letters,* XXXIX (September 27, 1572).

[15] *Op. cit.,* XLII (February 13, 1573).

[16] *Ibid.*

[17] "Learned men": in this context the word generally has the
sense of "theologians."

is conjoined with spirituality, cannot but have gained enormously from close and continuous contact with one who was pre-eminent in both. The incident, related by Teresa herself,[18] of the lesson in humility which John taught her by dividing the Host in giving her Communion is no doubt typical of many others never recorded. And in its way that simple narrative is as eloquent as the praise of her young companion which she pours out in her letters. Her "little Seneca," as she sometimes playfully called him, became, during those happy months in Ávila, "the father of her soul."[19] No words are too strong to express her admiration of him: "He is exceedingly holy;"[20] "Everyone considers him a saint;"[21] "He is a divine, heavenly man."[22] But it is her testimony to his personal influence upon her that is the most striking. "Since he left," she writes from Ávila, a year after his departure,

I have not found another like him in the whole of Castile, nor any that inspires such fervour in those that tread the way to Heaven. You would never believe how lonely I have been since he went. . . . I assure you that I should value it greatly if I had him here. . . . He is very spiritual and most experienced and learned. Those who were brought up here under his teaching miss him sorely.[23]

[18] St. Teresa: *Relations*, XXXV.
[19] St. Teresa: *Letters*, CCLXI (December 1578).
[20] *Op. cit.*, XLII (February 13, 1573).
[21] *Op. cit.*, CCX (January 16, 1578).
[22] *Op. cit.*, CCLXI (December 1578).
[23] *Ibid.*

An interesting question arises, too, concerning the writings of the two Saints. St. Teresa had long since written the majority of her works: *Life, Constitutions, Way of Perfection* and probably *Exclamations.* The *Conceptions of the Love of God* she wrote at about the time of St. John's sojourn in Ávila; the *Mansions* (or *Interior Castle*), perhaps her greatest work, was written in 1577—most of it in her own Ávilan convent of St. Joseph, while John was still at the Incarnation; the *Book of the Foundations*, which is the chief source for this chapter, was begun on August 24, 1573, during a visit to Salamanca, and no doubt much of it was written, perhaps with John at hand to refresh her memory, at the Incarnation. Did the constant talk which the two must have had about Teresa's books, or his reading or some of the works which had helped her, inspire John to begin writing himself? We cannot tell; but at least it can be said that down to this point he had probably written nothing, and it is very shortly after his leaving Ávila that some of his works are known to have been begun.[24]

[24] Cf. Baruzi, pp. 181-2; P. Bruno, p. 130.

CHAPTER III

Prison

T HE FIVE QUIET YEARS which John spent in Ávila were marked by the growth of dissensions between the religious of the Mitigated Rule and those of the Discalced Reform, a description of which forms a somewhat complicated and none too agreeable chapter of Carmelite history. Notwithstanding the extreme spirituality of the greatest and most saintly religious in sixteenth-century Spain, it has to be realized that the average level upon which the Orders lived, especially in the pre-Tridentine years, was by no means a high one. Again and again, in reading their chronicles, one seems to be in the midst of a family of wayward and quarrelsome children, whom a none too wise father or mother is unable to control. To enter into all the reasons for this state of things would involve too long a digression. It must suffice to remind the reader that, in religious history as well as in social and political, the sixteenth century and the twentieth were a long way apart—and that even the twentieth century is far from being perfect.

As we view these dissensions in distant retrospect, their two chief causes appear to have been the quite understandable misgivings of the friars of the Observance at the growth of a Reform in which, when it was first sanctioned, any tendency towards separation was strictly forbidden, and the large number of religious authorities to whom the one side or the other was able to appeal. Had there been one sole authority recognized by all, the friction occasioned by these misgivings might easily have subsided. But each party succeeded in marshalling its own particular champions, and the conflicts between the champions in their turn stimulated the rank and file, with results that can only be described as deplorable.

Though the dissensions can be traced as far back as the time of the birth of the Reform, they first came into the open when, in 1566, the General of the Order, Father Rubeo, an Italian, issued a censure of some of the Mitigated houses in Spain, and the Mitigated religious, complaining, without the General's knowledge, to the Pope, obtained from him, after the intervention of King Philip II, the transference of the control of the Spanish provinces to two Apostolic Visitors, who, being Dominicans, might be considered devoid of prejudice against them. The General retaliated by appointing "defenders" for the Order, presumably to preserve the balance of power. He need hardly have gone so far, however, for the Visitors began to give the Mitigated houses Discalced superiors; and finally the Visitor of the southern, or Andalusian, province, in which the foundation of Discalced houses had some time since been forbidden by the General, took the extraordinary course of resigning his powers into the hands of the Discalced friars. To the Mitigated this act must have seemed, not only irregular, but deliberately provocative, and they protested against it strongly. But their indignation reached a climax when in 1573 the office of Visitor was given to Fray Jerónimo Gracián, a Discalced friar only twenty-eight years of age and professed but six months previously.[1]

Fray Jerónimo, being another outstanding personality who was to enter prominently into the history of St. John of the Cross, must at this point be presented as clearly as is possible in a few sentences.[2] A brilliant young man, distinguished both as scholar and as organizer, becoming a Carmelite after nearly joining the Society of Jesus, he had personal gifts more notable still—frankness, suavity and charm of manner—which won him devotees everywhere. St. Teresa seems to have been captivated by him as she was by hardly anyone else, either earlier or later. "He is like an angel,"[3] she exclaimed—and she was a shrewd judge of character—shortly after first making his acquaintance. "Such gentleness, combined with perfection,"[4] she said, she had never seen. And although his precocity, his brilliance and what I have called elsewhere his "impatient energy"[5] made him

---

[1] Cf. *Studies*, II, 152.

[2] For a fuller estimate, see *Studies*, I, 238, II, 152-3.

[3] St. Teresa: *Letters*, LXXIV (June 12, 1575).

[4] *Op. cit.*, LXXII (May 12, 1575).

[5] *Studies*, II, 153.

powerful enemies, he retained her esteem all her life long.

The Mitigated friars appealed to the General against Gracián's appointment—a strange procedure, considering that their last appeal had been made to the Pope over his head. But Rubeo, though friendly to the Reform as such, disapproved strongly of the way in which these Visitors had been appointed, and therefore sought and obtained from the Holy See the revocation of their powers. Further, in May 1575, a General Chapter of the Carmelite Order, held at Piacenza, ordered the suppression of the Discalced houses which had been founded, in disobedience to Rubeo's authority, in Andalusia, and a Portuguese friar of the Mitigation, Father Tostado, was appointed to see that the suppression was carried into effect.

But if the Mitigation now had the General behind it, the Discalced had King Philip II, who thought highly of St. Teresa and esteemed the Reform from motives both of spirituality and of patriotism; they had also the Papal Nuncio, to whom they now appealed in their turn. The Nuncio did even more than was asked of him, not merely confirming Gracián's previous appointment as Visitor in Andalusia, but making him Apostolic Commissary over the Reform. Now this fell in with the ideas of St. Teresa, who believed that the only solution to the strife between the powerful Mitigation and the young and active Reform was that the latter should have a province of its own.[6] The counter-move, however, was not long in coming. In May 1576, Father Tostado, newly arrived in Spain, convened a meeting of the Priors of the Castilian Province. The Discalced Priors, who had been detained by the Nuncio, arrived late, only to find that the complete fusion of the Order had been decided upon[7]—which meant that Calced and Discalced would live together, each following his own rule.

This decision brought matters to a head. The King, as well as the Nuncio, took the part of Gracián, who resumed his duties in Andalusia but found some of the Mitigated houses in rebellion against his authority to the point of refusing him admittance. Thereupon, acting so impulsively that Teresa tried to dissuade him, he convened a Chapter of the Discalced at Almodóvar and established the Reform as a separate congregation. In the midst of all this, the Nuncio died, and his successor tried in vain to patch up the quarrel. But it was now too late: dissension had become civil war.

The war, which ended, in 1580, in the only possible way, with the permanent division of the Order, may be said to have been declared in 1577, when more or less polite diplomatic exchanges began to be succeeded by acts of a violence, often combined with puerility, which it is difficult to reconcile with the

[6] Cf. her letter (LXXVII) to Philip II, dated July 19, 1575.

[7] This statement is disputed (cf. P. Bruno, p. 148), but the authority on which it rests is a high one.

practices of the life of religion. When, for example, in October 1577, St. Teresa's three years' period of office as Prioress of St. Joseph's at Ávila came to an end, fifty-five out of the ninety-nine Calced nuns of the Incarnation voted for her return to them in that office. But the Provincial of the Mitigation, who was conducting the election, was determined that she should not return. Had it not been so pathetically unchristian the spectacle would have been farcical.[8] Surely, writes Teresa after the event, "such a thing has never before been seen."[9] Whenever a nun gave a vote in favour of Teresa, "he excommunicated her and abused her and pounded the papers with his fist and struck them and burned them. This happened a fortnight ago, but he has left these nuns without Communion and forbidden them to hear Mass or enter the choir, even when no office is being said there. Nobody is allowed to speak to them, not even their confessors or their parents."[10] On his next visit, the Provincial reassembled the nuns, announced that a new vote would be taken, and when "they replied that there was no reason to hold another election, since they had already held one," he re-excommunicated the fifty-five and made the minority elect another prioress, whom the majority thereupon refused to recognize except as sub-prioress. "I don't know

[8] "These affairs of ours are just like a comedy," Teresa had written in the preceding February (*Letters*, CLXXI: February 27-28, 1577).
[9] *Letters*, CXCVIII (October 1577).
[10] *Ibid.*

how it will end!"[11] sighed St. Teresa, in a vivacious narrative which at one moment seems to reveal her laughing at the childishness of the quarrel and at another weeping at the harm it was doing to religion. "If only they would leave me in peace!" she exclaims. "I have no desire to be in this Babylon."[12]

And neither had St. John of the Cross; but, sorely against his will, he was drawn into the very midst of the turmoil. For the first five years, from 1572 to 1577, he lived peaceably enough, in his little house near the Incarnation, and, except that he attended the Almodóvar Chapter, he seems to have viewed it all from afar. When the famous election at the Incarnation took place, he was still confessor there, and the fruitless attempt which he made to intervene brought the conflict nearer him. Nearer still it came when an attempt was made to induce him, with others, to abandon the Reform. Needless to say, he refused. The leaders of the Mitigation then attempted to employ compulsion.

On the night of December 3, the house where John and Germán lived was broken into, their papers were seized and they themselves were carried off to the monastery of the Observance in Ávila. After being "twice flogged and given all possible ill-treatment,"[13] they were removed to separate prisons,

[11] *Ibid.*
[12] *Ibid.*
[13] St. Teresa: *Letters*, CCVII (December 10, 1577), written a week after the event.

where, it was hoped, their spirit would be broken. Teresa, aghast at this high-handed act, took up her pen as soon as she heard of it and wrote a long letter to the King imploring his intervention. "I am terribly distressed to see our friars in such hands," she declared. "I would rather they were in the hands of the Moors: perhaps they would then meet with greater compassion. And as for this friar [John of the Cross], who is such a true servant of God, he is so weak, after all that he has suffered, that I fear for his life. For the love of Our Lord, I beseech Your Majesty forthwith to order his release."[14]

But, although he had previously intervened in the conflict with some effect, Philip seems now to have attempted, or accomplished, nothing. So John of the Cross, stripped of his rough frieze habit, which Teresa herself had made for him, and forced to don the cloth habit of the Mitigation, was taken from Ávila to Toledo, where Antonio, despite his years, had been confined during the previous summer. The journey of not less than eighty hilly miles was, for those days, a considerable one, and the brutality with which the victim was treated on the way made it the more trying. On reaching Toledo, he was blindfolded and taken to the monastery of the Mitigation, the most important and imposing in the entire Castilian Province. On the day after his arrival, he was interviewed by Father Tostado.

He took his stand, in a perfectly practical way,

---

[14] St. Teresa: *Letters*, CCIV (December 4, 1577).

upon the ground of legality. The Piacenza Chapter had made certain rules, and had empowered Tostado to enforce them, but he himself was holding and carrying out the duties of an office to which he had been appointed by the Apostolic Visitor, whose authority was superior to Tostado's, deriving directly from the Holy See. He might also have appealed to the authority of the late Nuncio, not to speak of that of Gracián, but the latter Tostado would not have recognized, while the former was now a thing of the past, though as a matter of fact the Nuncio's successor had, apparently with some reluctance, confirmed John's appointment.[15] Undoubtedly the multiplicity of authorities would have made it possible for either side in the dispute to produce impregnable arguments against the other. But, even when full consideration has been given to the omissions and mistakes of their supporters, the case of the Discalced must be recognized as the stronger and no one to-day would assert that John should have renounced his vows, disobeyed what he believed to have been a Divine command and abandoned a movement so spiritual in itself as well as so manifestly successful.

He remained resolute—as impervious to promises of high office if he would abandon the Reform as to threats of severe punishment if he would not. Dismissed by Tostado, he was sent back to his cell, where his period of trial began. The cell was ten

15 Cf. P. Bruno, pp. 164-5, 419-20.

feet by six—"hardly large enough to hold him," wrote Teresa, graphically, "small as he is."[16] It had no outside window—only a hole high in the wall connecting it with a large room which adjoined it. Except on the rare occasions when he was allowed a small oil lamp, the prisoner had to stand on a bench to get light enough to read his breviary, and even this was possible only when the sun was shining into a gallery at one end of the outer apartment. For the eight and a half months of his incarceration, which included the worst part of the hot Castilian summer, he had no change of clothing. His food was bread and water, with occasional scraps of salt fish. At first, he was made to eat this meal every evening on the floor of the refectory, after which he would bare his shoulders for the penance known as the "circular discipline." Sadistic as it sounds, this was as common a punishment at that time in religious houses as in-carceration. The friars would walk round him in a circle, each striking him with a whip as he passed, and handing it to the next in order. After a time they grew tired of this pastime, and indulged in it only twice or thrice weekly, then once weekly, and finally, from May onwards, at rare and irregular intervals. "Immovable as a rock"—the testimony comes from one of his persecutors[17] he endured it all in silence. "I don't know how God tolerates such things,"[18]

[16] St. Teresa: *Letters*, CCXLVI (August 1578). Cf. P. Silverio, I, 77, n. 2.
[17] Cf. P. Bruno, p. 170.
[18] *Ibid.*

wrote Teresa to Jerónimo Gracián long afterwards, when she heard of it. But John looked at it differently. "He that seeks not the Cross of Christ," he was to write in his *Maxims*, "seeks not the glory of Christ."[19] Not without reason had he re-named himself after the Cross.

Hoping, no doubt, that weakness and pain would break his spirit, the friars responsible for his incarceration kept visiting him in his cell, tormenting him with predictions that the Reform would shortly collapse and urging him to abandon it while there was still merit in so doing. To-day, perhaps, it is harder for us to imagine the sufferings of his mind than those of his body.[20] To physical pain, to hunger and to solitude long training had inured him, but had he ever before experienced mental torture comparable with this? His whereabouts, his sufferings and the constancy which he had shown to his ideals were all unknown to his friends; the cause to which he had dedicated his life, and for which he had already suffered so much, was in danger of extinction. Previously he had never been without the companionship and sympathy of those who shared his principles and all that he had undertaken had been rewarded with success. Now, for the first time, he was thrown back entirely upon God.

But this Toledan desert was yet to blossom as the rose. The earliest in date of those poems which, small

[19] "Points of Love," 23 (*Works*, III, 251).
[20] Cf. Baruzi, p. 189, n. 3.

in number as they are, have placed St. John of the Cross in the very first rank of Spanish writers are said on the highest authority to have had their birth in that prison cell. Among the few things which his gaolers permitted him were a little paper and ink, which he begged of them "because he wished to pass the time by composing a few things profitable to devotion."[21] When the paper came, he folded and re-folded it so as to make it into "a little book"; and in this book, which he took away with him when he left his prison, he wrote (as though to try his hand at verse composition) some simple doctrinal stanzas beginning *In principio erat Verbum.* Then, finding that they came easily, he composed a second poem, also simple in form but of great power and sensibility, introducing appropriately and for the first time one of the themes with which his name will always be associated, in the shape of a refrain "Although 'tis night." Finally,[22] he wrote the first thirty stanzas of the longest of his three superlatively great poems, the song of the soul pursuing the Divine Lover, entitled the "Spiritual Canticle."[23]

[21] Cf. P. Bruno, p. 426.

[22] There is no evidence for the order here given, but it is difficult to imagine any other.

[23] *Op. cit.*, p. 425. Cf. *Works*, III, 319. The phrase which justifies the use of the number "thirty" is "down to the stanza which says 'O nymphs of Judæa'." This, in the first redaction (*Works*, II, 29), is the opening phrase of Stanza 31 (cf. II, 444, note), but the sense would suggest that the writer stopped at the end of Stanza 30, with which the narrative comes to an end, the remaining stanzas being in the nature of reflections upon the narrative. The close of the poem, as we now have it, is rather an abrupt one.

If these were indeed the poems written in the Toledo cell (and the evidence is early in date and quite definite), the rapidity with which their author soared from the lowest level to the highest is remarkable. The doctrinal stanzas, or *romances*, written in a traditional Spanish form, are certainly no better than those of many a third-rate rhymester. Substituting rhyme for the device of assonance, more usual in verses of that type, he gives to every other line the monotonous ending—*ia*. His verses scan, but occasionally develop an awkward shamble. His language lacks the distinction which raises Newman's equally doctrinal "Praise to the Holiest" or even his "Firmly I believe and truly" so far above the level of the ordinary metrical hymn. The English version of the poem, which begins:

> Far away in the beginning
> Dwelt the Word of God on high,
> And in God His bliss eternal
> Had He everlastingly,[24]

is, if anything, flattering to the original, which is monotonous and unimaginative in the extreme.

The "Song of the soul that rejoices to know God by faith," on the other hand, with its *tema*:

> How well I know the fount that freely flows
> Although 'tis night,[25]

is not merely verse but poetry. Even technically its original shows a more marked advance upon the *ro-*

[24] *Works*, II, 455-6.
[25] *Op. cit.*, II, 454-5.

mances than can be accounted for by the poet's greater freedom of theme. With only two of the twenty-three lines[26] which, excluding the refrain, comprise the poem, can any fault be found at all. The remainder run quite smoothly; the rhymes are exact and vary with each stanza; the language has a dignity in perfect accord with the stateliness of the long line in which it is clothed. But more important than any of these qualities is the fact that the poem has genuine, though finely restrained, lyric emotion. Even with no knowledge of the conditions of its composition, one would divine that its author was a man of keen sensibility who had been through "a great storm of afflictions." Here, we say, is a poet of real promise: what could he not do but for the theological allegory which chains him to the ground?

The thirty stanzas of the "Spiritual Canticle," in which scholastic theology is exchanged for mystical, answer the question. Their beauty, even at a first reading, takes one's breath away. Many famous works have been written in prisons, but it would be difficult to find one so short which could rival this in its combination of religious fervour with literary grace. Never, perhaps, has the oft-told story of the Lover's quest of the Beloved been set in such exquisitely musical verse, to whose haunting melodies, some of them among the loveliest in Spanish literature, no translator can ever hope to do justice. An English

[26] I use P. Silverio's text, which rejects the second and the tenth of the stanzas translated in *Works, loc. cit.*

version, though it fails to convey the full force of such memorable phrases as "la soledad sonora," can give some idea of the heights to which the poet's imagination soared while his body lay in that dark cell: from the swiftness of the poem's movement, the vigour of its language, its skilful alternation of contrasting moods and the richness of its nature-images, some drawn from sacred or profane literature, others perhaps from the poet's own experience, one would deduce a youth full of life and energy, writing placidly in some country retreat, and deriving inspiration from the sights and sounds before his eyes. Never would one suspect a friar in his thirty-sixth year, prematurely aged by his ascetic life, bleeding, half starved, deprived for months of the sight of even a square of blue heaven and writing in close confinement and in all but total darkness:

> Lit by no earthly rays,
> Nay, only by heart's inmost fire ablaze

Impelled by that white-hot love of God, the little friar mounted up with wings like the eagle's, and, under the guise of a romantic love-story, which to a greater or a lesser degree would be intelligible to one who knew nothing of the Mystic Way, sketched with strong, nervous strokes the odyssey of the soul seeking her Beloved. Surely the idea of doing so must have been suggested to him by his own spiritual anguish. Surely on some evening, the shadows of the dark night of that prison must have merged into the deeper shadows of the Dark Night of the Soul, and his Calvary, like his Master's, have suddenly become a Calvary of despair as he felt the stab of that intolerable realization that he had lost the Divine companionship. Surely it was then that he raised his voice in that poignant cry: *¿A dónde te escondiste?*

> Whither hast vanishèd,
> Beloved, and hast left me full of woe?

When and how comfort came to him, we cannot say; but in some calmer moment he must have repeated those words to himself, and fashioned out of them the poem, of which they form the beginning:

> Whither hast vanishèd,
> Beloved, and hast left me full of woe,
> And like the hart hast sped,
> Wounding, ere thou didst go,
> Thy love, who follow'd, crying, high and low?

Twelve swiftly-moving stanzas describe the Bride's quest: her journey over hills and along streams; her appeal to the shepherds and even to forests and meadows:

> You meadow-land so green,
> Spangled with blossoms gay,
> Tell me, oh, tell me, has he pass'd your way?

The creatures answer that He has indeed passed, scattering gifts the while, but to the questing soul no mere reflection of God, no mere message from God suffices. She cries out for God Himself, and, at length, her long period of purgation is rewarded by a vision of light. The Spouse approaches and enraptures her. On returning to herself, she breaks into a paean of praise, searching in vain for a comparison with which to compare Him:

> My Love is as the hills,
> The lonely valleys clad with forest-trees,
> The rushing, sounding rills,
> Strange isles in distant seas,
> Lover-like whisperings, murmurs of the breeze.
>
> My love is hush-of-night,
> Is dawn's first breathings in the heav'n above,
> Still music veil'd from sight,
> Calm that can echoes move,
> The feast that brings new strength—the feast of love.

As the hymn proceeds, we find it foreshadowing, though at first only faintly, the joys of Union. The *lecho florido* ("Now blooms our nuptial bed . . ."), the Bride's deep drinking of the Beloved, the betrothal, the surrender, the solitude, the pasturing among the flowers. And finally the Beloved Himself takes up the tale; and, in what, when the poem left Toledo, was its conclusion, but in its completed form is but the beginning of a final *duo* between Lover and Beloved, describes the Bride's entry to Him

> Into the long'd-for garden, fair to sight.

How much of the allegorical interpretation of the "Spiritual Canticle" St. John of the Cross had in his mind when he first drafted the poem we cannot say; but so rich and so suggestive is the prose commentary upon it which he afterwards wrote that we may be sure each verb, each figure, each epithet was as carefully thought out as though it had belonged to a scientific treatise. Yet so completely effortless does the poem appear to be that any Spanish reader sensitive to art and unversed in mystical theology might be forgiven for supposing it to have been a purely spontaneous outpouring of lyrical genius. None the less, we have testimony coming, at second hand, from the poet himself that there was labour in it as well as inspiration. "The freshness of the words" in the "little book," attests a Beas nun, "together with their beauty and subtlety, caused me great wonder, and one day I asked him if God gave him those words which were so comprehensive and so lovely. And he answered: 'Daughter, sometimes God gave them to me and at other times I sought them.' "[27]

After the first five months of his imprisonment, John's treatment underwent some slight alleviation. Just at the time when the nightly floggings became only occasional, he was given a new and more compassionate gaoler, a young man, still under thirty, who was aghast at the state of his prisoner's health and the revolting conditions of his confinement, and so, when the friars were enjoying their midday *siesta*,

[27] *Works*, III, 319.

would open the door of his cell and allow him the relative freedom of the large room adjoining it.[28]

The possibility of escaping from his prison may have been suggested to John by his young gaoler's leniency with him, or by the news that, after three months' incarceration, Fray Germán had succeeded in escaping from the house where he had been immured at La Moraleja. At this point in his story, it is customary for the hagiographers to reproduce one narrative after another describing the supernatural visitations which he received from Our Lady. It was Assumption-tide, and it was natural enough that in his weak state he should dream of her or believe that she had appeared to him in person. It may indeed be that she did so, and, on the night of her festival, prophesied his immediate deliverance. It is almost easier to believe that a supernormal revelation should have shown him a way of escape than that, emaciated, starved and ill, with no previous knowledge of the monastery, he should have discovered one unaided. But just as little Juan de Yepes, when he had fallen into the water, had had a vision of a beautiful lady, but was fished out by a passing peasant, so, without denying the genuineness of anything that may have been seen by Father John of the Cross, we cannot but suspect that a large part in his successful escape was played by the kindly gaoler.

The contemporary testimonies, for obvious rea-

[28] This evidence comes from the young gaoler himself, whose name was Fray Juan de Santa María (P. Silverio, I, 78-9).

sons, do not assert this. It was the Blessed Virgin, they tell us, who showed him the convenient window and instructed him in picking the locks of the doors leading from his cell and from the outer apartment. But did one who as a boy had been apprenticed to a carpenter need such instruction? The more pertinent question is: Who provided him with the screwdriver? It is suggestive that, according to his gaoler's own subsequent evidence, his prisoner had bestowed on him his most precious possession—a crucifix which had been given him by Teresa—had thanked him for his kindnesses and had begged his forgiveness for any trouble that he might have caused him. Can this young friar have been so young as not to recognize a valedictory address when he heard it? He was already allowing him still greater liberty—a few minutes' walk beyond the outer room every day. Was it not in one of those walks that John saw an open window overlooking the river Tagus? Did not his gaoler leave the doors unlocked one night after his return? In any case, it is clear that his actual escape, made probably on the night of August 16, 1578, was due principally to his own shrewdness. When his cell-door was bolted, says one contemporary account, "God inspired him to insert his finger, and thus it was not secured."[29] Then, having made a rope from strips of his bedclothes, he opened his door at dead of night, tiptoed through the outer apartment, where two friars who had arrived on a

[29] *Works*, III, 342.

visit were uneasily sleeping, made his way to the window which he had discovered during his earlier reconnaissances, and let himself down, hoping that the rope would take him safely to the ground.

It did not,[30] and the prisoner had to jump a distance of nine feet. Picking himself up, he discovered that he was in an open space between the Carmelite house of his incarceration and an unknown convent. Stealthily he made his way to the one haven which awaited him in Toledo—the Reformed convent founded by Teresa ten years earlier. It was not long before his captors found the rope hanging from the window-sill and learned of their victim's flight. The young gaoler was sent for, affirmed that he had duly locked the prison doors on the evening before and suggested that the exploit must have been miraculous. The friars seem to have accepted this explanation, but they were not credulous enough to allow the gaoler to escape some of the customary penalties, though sparing him the whole of them. Certain Carmelite commentators have been scathingly critical of biographers who have queried the miraculous element in the story: they might have spared some of their censure for the Toledo friars, who made the poor gaoler suffer for what they accepted as supernatural.

The scene in that convent at dawn can be imagined. Few such excitements could fall to the lot of a

[30] There are slight discrepancies between the various accounts of this part of the narrative. Cf. *Works*, III, 341-8, *passim*.

house of Discalced nuns in a generation. Hardly had
the fugitive arrived and been given a light meal than
the friars of the Mitigation appeared on the scene,
to enquire "with all due discretion" if he were there.
The portress, "who had even more discretion than
they, answered them excellently, without lying, but
leaving them puzzled as to whether the nuns had
seen any religious."[31] Meanwhile a Canon of the
Cathedral was sent for, and, eluding the sentries
whom the friars had placed round the house, got him
out by way of a small door in the convent chapel
which they had omitted to picket, and, after pro-
viding him with fresh clothes, sent him away where
he would be safe.

Short as was the time which he spent in the convent, however, he occupied himself by edifying the
nuns in a way which posterity delights to remember.
Several accounts of the occurrence testify that he
took some of the sisters with him into the convent
chapel, and there recited to them the stanzas which
he had composed in his prison,[32] and which "appeared to be written" (as he himself diffidently put
it, at a later date) "with a certain degree of fervour of
love for God."[33] The witnesses, testifying thirty-six
years after the event, do not agree as to exactly which
these verses were, but there is no mistaking the
authenticity of the picture which they combine to

[31] *Works*, III, 342.
[32] *Works*, III, 354, 356.
[33] Preface to *Spiritual Canticle* (*Works*, II, 23).

give of the little friar reciting his poems in the convent chapel, his body frail and torn, his voice perhaps weak and trembling but his eyes aglow with the passion of Divine love.

CHAPTER IV

Beas and Monte Calvario

Twice, during his comparatively short life of forty-nine years, St. John of the Cross was plunged into the dark night of physical and mental suffering: once, by the friars of the Mitigated Rule which he had renounced soon after the beginning of his career, and once by the friars of the very Reform which he had been so largely instrumental in promoting. These two experiences may be considered strangely symbolic of two of the most characteristic features of his description of the Mystic Way—the Dark Night of Sense and the "more horrible and awful" Dark Night of the Spirit. But, as the second period of suffering came near the end of his life, the first stands out the more prominently in his history, which it cuts very decisively into two. Before his imprisonment, he had travelled but little and his activities were confined within a very small area of Old Castile; immediately after his escape, he went south, into Andalusia, where he spent the fourteen years of life that remained to him in journeyings comparable with those of St. Teresa, and where he died. Before his imprisonment, nothing had been heard of him as a writer; so far as is known, most of his verse and all his prose was written during those last few years, and amid unusual activity of body, mind and spirit.

John's southward journeys began as soon as he left the house of the hospitable Canon of Toledo. Weak as he. was, he had been allowed, no more than a month after his escape from prison, to travel to Almodóvar del Campo, some thirty miles south-west of Ciudad Real, and due south of Toledo, where an important Chapter of the Reform had been summoned for October 9. "I am distressed that they have allowed him to go," wrote the solicitous and motherly Teresa, in mid-September. "Please God he may not die of it."[1] But the fault may well have been in the determination of John himself. The affairs of the Discalced had improved but little during his imprisonment. True, the General died about this time,[2] and as on his death Tostado's commission automatically came to an end, the friars of the Observance had perforce to cool their ardour. On the other hand, Gracián had been acting rashly. Instead of being content to petition for the separation of the two branches of the Order, he had spurned the advice of Teresa and done what would have been appropriate only if this separation had already been granted. Exactly one week after the meeting of the Almodóvar Chapter, the Papal Nuncio retaliated by issuing a decree which made the Reform subject to the Ob-

[1] St. Teresa: *Letters*, CCXLVII (September 1578).
[2] For the date, see P. Silverio, I, 87 and P. Bruno, p. 190.

servance, and sent both the old pioneer, Antonio of Jesus, and the young leader, Jerónimo Gracián, into exile. Soon after this, we find John riding still farther southward, on his way to the monastery of Monte Calvario, where the Chapter had appointed him Vicar during its Prior's absence in Rome.

Precisely what was the significance of this appointment it is impossible to determine. Most probably it aimed at giving him a period of tranquillity for physical recuperation, at sending him out of the reach of his persecutors and at isolating him from a conflict which was unlikely to be resolved for some time. At any rate, those were its actual consequences. Recuperation was aided by a stay *en route* at Beas de Segura, a peaceful village situated on a tributary of the Guadalimar, an oasis in the mountainous wastes of the Sierra Morena. Here, three and a half years previously, St. Teresa had founded a convent of the Discalced, the prioress of which was one of her most beloved spiritual daughters, the Venerable Anne of Jesus.

We may well believe that John and Anne "understood each other" as readily and as completely as had John and Teresa eleven years earlier. They were much of an age, highly educated and united in a common love for the Mother Foundress. They spoke the same spiritual language. Others of the nuns—and the community seems to have been an exceedingly gracious and spiritual one—have left on record the depth of the impression which the saint—for as a saint they already thought of him—made upon them. One gives a typical description of how he alone was able to relieve her long-standing spiritual distress. "He understood me at once," it ends, "and gave me assurance for my journey and courage to suffer what I had still to bear." Then it adds—and one can almost hear the note of pride in the youthful voice: "He called me 'My daughter Mary' and I gloried in having such a father."[3]

Beas is a milestone in John's life, as well as a resting-place, for it is during his stay there that we catch the first hint of his having been writing in prose. Nearly the whole of his literary work consists of extensive commentaries on his three greatest poems— the "Spiritual Canticle" of the Toledo prison, and the two "Songs of the Soul" known respectively, from their first lines, as "Dark Night" and "Living Flame of Love." Perhaps he had already conceived the project of writing an exposition of the "Spiritual Canticle"—or can this idea have come to birth in the tranquil solitudes of Beas? It might even have been suggested to him by some of those appreciative sisters.[4] For here, just as in the chapel of the Toledo convent, he recited these stanzas—not now trembling and exhausted, but rested in body, and as full of serenity in his body as in his spirit. Yet, wonderful as this experience must have been for the Beas nuns, it

[3] For a fuller quotation from this testimony, see P. Bruno, p. 194.

[4] As one of them says was in fact the case. "Some of the expositions were written at Beas, as answers to questions put to him by the nuns" (*Works*, III, 319).

did not leave them satisfied. Questions came to their lips as they listened, and these questions John answered, until at last he must have found himself embarking upon a commentary almost without knowing it. Some seven years later, when the then Prioress, Catherine of Jesus, lay dying, she asked for these stanzas to be sung to her, so greatly had she been impressed by their exposition.

All available evidence points to the closeness of the tie between these nuns and their unofficial confessor. Though his stay at Beas was short ("a few days"), for he had to go on to the neighbouring hermitage-monastery of Monte Calvario, in the hills above the valley, he used to walk back there, on Saturdays and on the vigils of great festivals, sometimes as frequently as once a week, for the purpose of continuing his instructions and hearing confessions. Even after leaving Monte Calvario, he visited them from time to time, and, when distance forbade this, he would write to them. "He used often to say that there were none whom he loved so much as the nuns of Beas."[5]

Monte Calvario is the first of the houses in which St. John of the Cross lived for any length of time and concerning which stories of his activities have come down to us. It is here that he is said to have made his

[5] Deposition, *cit.* Baruzi, p. 200, n. 1. This critic reminds us that, of John's eighteen extant letters, eight are addressed either to individual members of this community or to the community as a whole.

original sketch-map of the Mount of Perfection, which illustrates his commentary *The Ascent of Mount Carmel*.[6] His leisure, one witness tells us, he would employ in carving wooden figures of Christ[7]— and we know from his commentaries that wood-carving, though he never took it up as a profession, was of keen interest to him.[8] But he must have spent much more of it in writing. For at Monte Calvario, we may be almost certain, he was at work on his commentaries. For one thing, the various copies of his sketch-map, which he would make for the Beas nuns to place as bookmarks in their breviaries,[9] contain phrases from the *Ascent of Mount Carmel*; for another, these nuns used to take notes on the instructions he gave them, and an extract from the notes, as reproduced by one of the nuns, is almost exactly identical with a celebrated passage in that treatise.[10] Further, this same witness says that "some of the expositions" to the early stanzas of the *Spiritual Canticle* "were written at Beas, as answers to questions put to him by the nuns," and that "he also occasionally wrote spiritual things that were of great benefit."[11] The progression is exactly what one would expect: first, either with or without any idea

[6] See frontispiece to *Works*, Vol. 1.

[7] Cf. Baruzi, p. 70, n. 4.

[8] Cf. *Ascent of Mount Carmel*, III, xxxvi-xxxvii (*Works*, I, 315-17).

[9] *Works*, III, 320.

[10] The phrases (*Works*, III, 321-2) should be compared with *Ascent of Mount Carmel*, I, xiii (*Works*, I, 60-2).

[11] *Works*, III, 319-20.

of interpreting them, he writes some poems; next, he recites them; then he answers questions about them; then commits his answers to paper; and finally collects these answers and begins a systematic and connected commentary.

The *Ascent of Mount Carmel,* which may be taken as having been begun at Monte Calvario, is based upon the poem "Dark Night," which some critics believe to have been composed,[12] together with an undistinguished verse paraphrase of the psalm *Super flumina Babylonis,*[13] in the Toledo prison. On internal evidence (and, external testimony being inconclusive, there is little else to go upon, beyond surmise) it would seem more probable that the poem was written soon after the author's escape. Consider those first phrases of "Dark Night," so blunt and matter-of-fact in the original Spanish—

> En una noche oscura
>
> · · · ·
>
> Salí sin ser notada,
> Estando ya mi casa sosegada—

(On a dark night . . . I went out without being observed, my house being now at rest.)

Is it not likely that those phrases were written down by their author as an exact and literal description of his escape and that he built upon them the narrative which follows much as he built the "Spiritual Can-

[12] *Works,* III, 353-4.
[13] *Works,* III, 358.

ticle" upon the cry wrung from him by some poign‑
ant moment of distress? The more often I read the
poem, the more probable seems to me this theory of
its origin.

Its theme is that of the "Spiritual Canticle": the
mystic quest. But it is only one-fifth the length of the
other poem and the theme is treated more concisely
and with more conscious art. The perfection of these
liras,[14] indeed, is another argument in favour of their
having been written at a later date than those of the
longer poem, and at a period of greater mental
serenity than the author could have enjoyed in his
prison. The lines are among the most flawless and
the most melodious in Spanish literature. The emo‑
tional and artistic force of the ejaculation "O mo‑
ment of delight!" which gives its tone to the first two
stanzas; the magnificent apostrophe to night, in the
fifth; the boldness with which the poet transfers the
properties of light to darkness; the graceful interplay
of broad, dark vowels and the delicate feminine ca‑
dences contrasting with the vigour of the phraseology
and the theme—all these are qualities which I have
stressed elsewhere, though some of them lose their
potency in translation. But translation will not ob‑
scure another of the poem's merits—the perfection
of its architecture. As in the conflict of a drama, the
emotional tone rises till it reaches the fifth stanza, in

[14] The *lira*, a five-lined stanza in which both these poems are
written, is a form introduced into Spanish poetry not long previ‑
ously by Garcilaso de la Vega (cf. *Works*, III, 18; Baruzi, pp. 113ff.;
Studies, I, 269, note).

which occurs the poem's culminating moment:
thereafter, the emotion continues on a lower but
well-sustained level until it sinks to rest in a melodious cadence which in the original gives the impression of complete finality:

> Entre las azucenas olvidado.
> (Amid the lilies drowning all my care.)

The narrative of the quest does little more than
hint at the Purgative Way but dwells with evident
delight upon the Illuminative—then, in the cul-
minatory stanza, passes suddenly to the Life of
Union, upon which it stays till its close. The figures
of speech in the first part of the poem are few and
simple: the night, the ladder, the burning light. The
second part, on the other hand, is one continuous
figure, based largely on the *Song of Songs*. It is as
though the author renounced in advance all attempts
to describe any aspect of the Unitive Life otherwise
than allegorically: we shall find him adopting the
same procedure later in the "Living Flame of Love,"
which, as he himself said in the preface to his commentary upon it, relates "to things so interior and
spiritual that words commonly fail to describe
them."[15]

There was not the same difficulty in commenting
the early stanzas of "Dark Night," and it is interesting to observe that, although the Saint began two
books upon the poem, *The Ascent of Mount Carmel*

[15] *Works*, III, 15.

and *Dark Night of the Soul*, he left both uncompleted. The former is much the longer, and much less of a commentary upon his poems than anything else he ever wrote. For, whereas the *Spiritual Canticle* follows its text stanza by stanza, and deals conscientiously with each phrase of each stanza, making few digressions, the *Ascent of Mount Carmel* departs from its text almost immediately. Of its three books, the first sets out to interpret the first stanza, but, after devoting twelve chapters to the four opening words, it polishes off the remainder of the stanza in barely two pages. The second book begins by explaining the general sense of the second stanza, but then forgets all about the poem, which neither here nor in the third book is heard of again. Hardly more than one-fifth of the *Ascent*, in fact, is in the narrower sense of the word a commentary at all.

But we must not ascribe this departure from the exegetical method to the author's impatience. Just as a mere phrase or a single experience, inspired by his genius, blossomed into a masterpiece of poetry, so one simple stanza of one of his own poems served him as starting-point for a masterly treatise on ascetic and mystical theology.

It is curious that, whereas the poem is concerned almost exclusively with Illumination and Union, the commentary should treat solely of Purgation. The fact is that the key to the book is to be found, not in the text of the poem at all, but in the twofold interpretation of the word "night," "which spiritual persons call purgations or purifications of the soul; . . . in both of them the soul journeys, as it were, by night, in darkness."[16] In the first of his three books the author deals with the Night of Sense, and in the second and third with active purgation in the Night of Spirit. His intention had been to devote a fourth book to passive purgation in the Night of Spirit, but the third book, after wandering considerably from its main theme (to the great edification of the reader), breaks off abruptly and brings the work to an end.

The first book shows signs of having been written with particular care. Despite the sublimity of his own religious experience, St. John of the Cross, as we shall see again, is always most solicitous for those who by comparison with himself are beginners, and nowhere can we find greater insight, penetration and clarity of expression than in this purely instructional treatise. Its main theme being mortification, a great part of it is taken up with the weaning of the soul from sensual desire, and the chapters on desire lead up to the entry into the Night of Sense, described in Chapter XIII—perhaps the most famous piece of prose that St. John of the Cross ever wrote. After describing the active and the passive aspect of this act of purgation, he gives the soul those well-known counsels which some have declared to be counsels of perfection, and which, with their stark antitheses, strike terrors into all but the most resolute:

[16] *Works*, I, 18. For the division of the work see I, lviii-lix, 18 n.

Strive always to choose, not that which is easiest, but
that which is most difficult;
Not that which is most delectable, but that which is
most unpleasing;
Not that which gives most pleasure, but rather that
which gives least, *etc.*[17]

And these are followed by some lines which the
author wrote beneath the diagram of the "Mount of
Perfection" already referred to, and reproduced in
the *Ascent of Mount Carmel*:

In order to arrive at having pleasure in everything,
Desire to have pleasure in nothing, *etc.*[18]

The second and third books, which describe active
purgation in the Night of the Spirit, are considerably
more discursive than the first: indeed, the finest and
clearest descriptions of this second Night, incomparably "more horrible and awful"[19] than the first,
"wherein the soul is purged and stripped according
to the spirit, and subdued and made ready for the
union of love with God," are to be found, not in the
Ascent at all, but in its much later continuation, the
Dark Night of the Soul. The second book of the
Ascent begins with an exposition of the virtue of
faith, which the author equates with the second
Night, goes on to discuss the progress from meditation to contemplation, and then, entering upon
active purgation of the understanding, takes up at

[17] *Works*, I, 61.
[18] *Works*, I, 62-3.
[19] *Works*, I, 371.

length the subject of visions, locutions and other types of supernatural revelation. The third book deals systematically with active purgation of the memory and the will, but finds space also to discuss such practical subjects as the devotional use of images, the furnishing of oratories, the celebration of religious festivals, the abuse of ceremonial and the qualities of a good sermon. The author has just observed that "eloquent language" and "a good style and gestures" are less important in a preacher than spirituality, and added that he does not of course intend "to condemn good style and rhetoric and phraseology," when, for some unknown reason, and in the middle of a sentence, the treatise comes to an end.

CHAPTER V

Baeza and Granada

AFTER SPENDING EIGHT MONTHS at Monte Calvario, John was sent to Baeza, a Cathedral city about forty miles to the south-west, where, on June 14, 1579, he began a fresh task, the direction of a newly-established Carmelite College, the type of foundation of which he had already had experience at Alcalá de Henares. Here, once again, the good-will of the Beas nuns followed him, the Prioress giving him "no little help with letters to persons of importance, both ecclesiastical and law;"[1] and, only "a few days" after his arrival, he went all the way back to Beas to pay them another visit. He was much less happy at Baeza —a city of considerable size—than he had been in the country. For there he first came into contact with Andalusians in the mass; and, like most good Castilians, he disliked them intensely. "He cannot endure these people," wrote Teresa to Gracián[2]—and she herself shared his opinion. In uncongenial society he experienced loneliness of a kind which he had never known in solitude, the keener by contrast with the happiness of Monte Calvario and Beas. At Baeza he described himself as "in exile . . . and alone," and

[1] *Works*, III, 322-3.
[2] St. Teresa, *Letters*, CCCLVIII (March 23-24, 1581).

added, in quite a Pauline sentence, with a curious mixture of whimsical humour and pathos, "for since I was swallowed by that whale [*i.e., the Toledan prison*] and cast up in this strange harbour, I have not been found worthy to see you again, nor the saints that are up yonder [*i.e., in Castile*]."[3] So completely detached as a rule is St. John of the Cross from human preferences that this unexpected manifestation of frailty produces in the reader as much a shock of surprise as a glow of sympathy.

At the time of which we are speaking, the city of Baeza had a University; and, like the students at Alcalá—and as John himself had done at Salamanca —the students of the Carmelite College would take the University courses. In re-entering an academic milieu, we may suppose, he found a certain degree of compensation for what he had lost. He "organized the study of Scholastic Theology in the College . . . sometimes presiding at the students' exercises and sometimes taking part in the disputations,"[4] not only with the students, but with learned doctors from the University, who, on other occasions also, engaged with him in Biblical and theological discussions. We need not, however, detail the abundant eulogies of the "profound wisdom" of this "Divine oracle" which both students from the College and doctors from the University have left on record.[5]

[3] Letter to M. Catalina de Jesús: July 6, 1581 (*Works*, III, 264).
[4] Baruzi, p. 208, n. 1.
[5] P. Bruno, p. 214.

More convincing testimonies than these can be found in his extant writings.

There is evidence that, while at Baeza, John composed four more stanzas of the "Spiritual Canticle," and it may not be fanciful to connect the invitation in the first of them:

> Hide thee, my lover dear,
> And lift thine eyes until the hills they see . . .[6]

with the superb view of the southern *sierra* beyond the Guadalquivir, or to allow another of them to remind us that their author was in the habit of going out for days on end into the solitude of the country:[7]

> So she who dwelt alone
> In loneliness again has built her nest,
> Guided alone by one,
> Upon her lonely quest,
> Who, lonely too, by love was sorely prest.[8]

But for the most part he seems to have written prose rather than verse at Baeza—more of the expositions of the stanzas of the "Canticle" and perhaps more of the *Ascent of Mount Carmel*. Probably his position as Rector of the College left him less time than he would have liked for writing. Nor was his work solely among students. He was as much concerned about the ninety and nine as in the days when he

[6] *Works*, II, 447.

[7] P. Bruno, p. 216.

[8] *Works*, II, 447. The repetition in each stanza of the syllable "lone" parallels the more sonorous repetition in the original of "soledad . . . solas."

went out from the "little house" at Duruelo and spent long days in evangelization. And, both by precept and by example, he inspired others. When he was at Baeza, says a contemporary record, confessors, though busy day and night, found it difficult to cope with the penitents who flocked to them.[9] A different picture, this, from that of the hermit-existence at Monte Calvario.

The two years or more which John spent at Baeza were marked by one most important development in the history of the Discalced Reform. The decree of October 16, 1578, which made the Discalced subject to their brethren of the Observance, could not possibly be implemented, so strong and active had the Reform already become and so certain was it of survival. Its leaders were convinced that the only satisfactory solution of the trouble between the two branches of the Order would be their complete separation. In the last phase of the struggle Philip II appears to have taken the initiative and to have won over the Nuncio, Sega, who had been so much harder on the Discalced than his predecessor. During 1579 we find him gradually coming round to a recognition of the great work they were doing, while, at Rome, representatives of the Reform were striving earnestly to obtain Papal intervention. This object was attained on June 22, 1580, when a Bull of Gregory XIII established the Discalced as a separate province. On March 3, 1581, the first Chapter of the Discalced

[9] P. Bruno, p. 222.

Province was held at Alcalá, and Gracián, who since
the issue of the Bull had been acting as Vicar-General, was elected Provincial, though by a majority of
only one. None can have been happier now than the
Mother of the Reform, St. Teresa. The triumph of
her cause, the election of her dearly beloved disciple,
and the zeal and success with which, in the months
following, he established new Discalced foundations
forming a fitting climax to more than twenty years
of incessant activity. On October 15, 1582, Teresa
died. She had seen her "little Seneca" for the last
time in the previous November.

St. John of the Cross, who had of course attended
the Alcalá Chapter, was appointed by it to a post still
farther south than Baeza, the priorate of the monastery of Los Mártires, near Granada. His feelings
when he heard of the appointment, if he allowed
himself to have any, must have been curiously
mingled. It would mean a complete abandonment
of an academic environment which, being the scholar
that he was, he must have loved, and yet it would be
restoring to him that even more beloved solitude in
which he found his greatest companionship. It would
free him from the company of the Baezanos, whom
he disliked so much that he had begged Teresa to
use her influence against his re-appointment to the
College—yet would the Granadinos prove any better? On the other hand, again, Los Mártires was not
a busy city like Baeza; and, although the change
would take him farther from his own Castile and

into the very depths of the south, the greater degree of isolation might bring him into less close and frequent contact with southerners. But probably he felt the outstanding feature of the change to be the distance it would take him from Beas.

During his two years at Baeza, he had still managed occasionally to visit the Beas nuns, though less frequently than was possible from Monte Calvario. Even Granada did not cut him off from them entirely. Though it was nearly one hundred miles south of Baeza and the greater part of the way lay across the rough, wild *sierras*, he contrived from time to time either to make a special journey there or to combine it with one of the other journeys occasioned by his position as Prior or by the later office which he held of Vicar-Provincial of Andalusia. It was at Beas that he wrote the final stanzas of the "Spiritual Canticle." One of the sisters, questioned by him about her devotions, replied that she spent her hours of prayer in the contemplation of God's beauty and greatness. Soon after this he left, but on his next visit he brought her the first of these stanzas:

> Belovèd, let us sing,
> And in thy beauty see ourselves portray'd,
> Where purest waters spring
> Rippling o'er hill and glade;
> Then enter farther in the forest's shade.[10]

And one would like to think that the nun's simple reply also inspired that lovely passage from the commentary:

[10] *Works*, II, 447. Baruzi, p. 214, n. 5.

... and thus I shall see Thee in Thy beauty, and Thou wilt see me in Thy beauty; and Thou wilt see Thyself in me in Thy beauty, and I shall see myself in Thee in Thy beauty; and thus I may be like to Thee in Thy beauty, and Thou mayest be like to me in Thy beauty, and my beauty may be Thy beauty, and Thy beauty my beauty; and I shall be Thou in Thy beauty, and Thou wilt be I in Thy beauty, because Thy beauty itself will be my beauty.[11]

It must, at any rate, have been at this time that the Saint mounted to the height of his inspiration, penetrated "even to the caverns of the rocky mine" and penned those last stanzas, which with the imagery of Union:

> Enter we, thou and I,
> Those secret haunts divine. . . .
>
> There unto this thy dove
> That which her soul has yearn'd for wilt thou
>   show. . . .
>
> The gently moving air;
> The sweetest song of Philomel. . . .[12]

culminating in that curiously abrupt change of metaphor, and that ending, which, if considered apart from its interpretation, is no ending at all:

> ... For the long, long siege is o'er
> And the horsemen, halting here,
> Dismount and gaze upon the water clear.[13]

[11] *Works*, II, 164.
[12] *Works*, II, 447.
[13] *Ibid.*

It was not till January 20, 1582, that John arrived to take up his duties at Los Mártires, accompanied by a number of other Carmelites, chief among them Anne of Jesus, who had been appointed head of a new foundation at Granada, to begin its work in the house of Doña Ana de Peñalosa, for whom St. John of the Cross later wrote that superb treatise, *Living Flame of Love*. He resided at Los Mártires continuously for two years and intermittently for four years more. The monastery stood on what was then a bare hill near the Palace of the Alhambra, and bareness was apparently also the chief trait of the monastery cupboards. In such straits was it that the new Prior had to go out with a companion and beg for bread. He also took part in the building which was going on when he arrived, mixing the sand and lime and making bricks like any labourer. The community had been in existence for nine years, but all this time had occupied a single isolated house. A second house had already been built and a reservoir constructed for the supply of necessary water. The additions made in John's time were some further buildings, an aqueduct and a cloister.

Besides managing the material and spiritual affairs of his own monastery, John acted as confessor and director to Anne of Jesus and her Carmelites, and Anne, after Teresa's death, seems to have become his closest friend. To her we owe the first copies, completed in 1584, of the commentary on the "Spiritual Canticle." The "Canticle" itself, as we have seen, was well known to the Beas nuns, and Anne now requested its author to complete and put into circulation his exposition of it, parts of which were no doubt also known to them, at least in substance. In his preface to the commentary, which contains the famous description of the stanzas, already alluded to, as "appearing to be written with a certain degree of fervour of love for God," he sets himself only the aim of "touching upon and expounding some points and effects of prayer" and disclaims any intention of revealing "all the breadth and plenteousness embodied in the fertile spirit of love." He also pays a tribute to Anne's spiritual progress. Reminding her that in this commentary he is not as a rule writing for beginners, he continues:

To Your Reverence Our Lord has granted the favour of drawing you forth from these beginnings and leading you farther onward into the bosom of His Divine love. Thus I trust that, although I write here of certain points of scholastic theology concerning the interior commerce of the soul with its God, it may not be in vain to have talked somewhat after the manner of pure spirit; for, though Your Reverence may lack the practice of scholastic theology, wherein are comprehended Divine verities, you lack not that of mystical theology, which is the science of love, and wherein these verities are not only known but also experienced.[14]

This and the other commentaries John wrote in his cell, we are told, with the aid of no books save the Bible ("almost all of which he knew by heart"), a

[14] *Works*, II, 25

Flos Sanctorum and an occasional volume which he might borrow from the library and was in the habit of returning as soon as he had used it.[15] To gather this from external testimony is not in the least surprising. The commentaries, though full of well-digested learning, contain few direct quotations from anything but Scripture. As a young man John had read widely and can hardly have failed to keep up his studies: St. Augustine, St. Bernard, St. Thomas, St. Gregory the Great, the pseudo-Dionysius, the Victorines, Ruysbroeck and Tauler are among the authors with whom it is either quite certain or highly probable that he was familiar. But his learning had all been thoroughly digested and assimilated till it had become part of the writer.[16]

The *Spiritual Canticle*, says P. Juan Evangelista, who was the closest friend of St. John of the Cross during the last three years of his life, "was the first thing that he wrote."[17] If we take "wrote" to mean "completed" (for the *Ascent*, says the witness, might have been begun earlier)[18] that is definite and probably conclusive information. The same witness tells us that all the other commentaries were written at Granada also. "I saw him write all of them," he deposes, "for, as I have said, I was ever at his side. The *Ascent of Mount Carmel* and *Dark Night* he wrote here, in this house, at Granada, little by little,

[15] *Works*, III, 376; Baruzi, p. 148, nn. 3-4.
[16] P. Crisógono, I, 29ff.; Baruzi, pp. 134ff.
[17] *Works*, III, 376.
[18] *Works*, III, 379.

for he was able to proceed with his work only with many interruptions. The *Living Flame of Love* he also wrote in this house, when he was Vicar Provincial . . . and this he wrote in a fortnight, when he was busy with many other things."[19] A later deposition, which modifies the statement about the *Ascent of Mount Carmel* to the extent indicated above, is even more emphatic about the other books. The *Canticle* and *Living Flame* "he wrote here, for he began and ended them in my time." The *Dark Night* "he certainly wrote here . . . for I saw him write part of it; this is certain, for I saw it."[20] If we accept this evidence and its author's deductions from it—and, save that the evidence on the *Dark Night* is inconclusive, there seems no reason to do otherwise—we must think of the whole of the leisure of those six years, the latter of them so much cut into by travel, as having been spent upon the commentaries. Granada, then, completed what Toledo, Beas, Monte Calvario and Baeza had begun.

The *Dark Night of the Soul* is, in fact, if not in intention, that fourth book of the *Ascent of Mount Carmel* which was to treat of passive purgation. If the Saint, while at Granada, really completed the *Ascent* and went straight on to write the *Dark Night*, the concluding pages of the *Ascent* must have disappeared. But it is more probable that, while writing the somewhat matter-of-fact chapter on preaching,

[19] *Works*, III, 376.
[20] *Works*, III, 379.

he suddenly felt inspired to turn to the subject of the soul's passivity, and so laid the *Ascent* aside, meaning to come back to it, which he never did. The adoption of a fresh name for what was to have been the fourth book of the other treatise no doubt expresses the author's sense of its importance, which is fully justified both by its contents and by its execution.

Like the *Ascent*, the *Dark Night* is incomplete, glossing—more systematically than its predecessor—only two of the poem's eight stanzas. It is the maturer work of the two. Though nearly three-quarters of it deals with the rarest form of spiritual desolation, which comes only to the most advanced contemplatives, the clarity and the precision of the author's expositions leave nothing to be desired. No other writer, in this respect, has surpassed him: for a description of the Dark Night of the Spirit it is to this book that we invariably turn.

It cannot be doubted that here, as elsewhere in his writings, St. John of the Cross is drawing upon his own mystical experiences and translating them into the objective and scholarly language which came naturally to one of his temperament and training. This accounts for the skill with which he threads his way through the intricacies of language and avoids the pitfalls of illuminism and quietism into which some of his not too benevolent commentators would have liked to thrust him. The sixteenth chapter of the second book, which "explains how, though in darkness, the soul walks securely," is a masterpiece of clarity, rivalling even the exposition of the first stanza in the fourth to the eighth chapters of the same book, which P. Silverio calls "brilliant beyond all description."[21] And yet, even with the burden of such lofty expositions upon his mind, the Saint never forgets the "beginner" struggling in the Night of Sense. Nowhere better than in the first book of the *Dark Night* does he show his deep and complete understanding of human nature. Gently yet firmly he probes spiritual imperfections concealed by apparent virtue, reveals their sources and prescribes for their eradication. And, always tactful and never in the least censorious, he testifies to the genuineness of his own experience and to his truly saint-like humility.

The last of his commentaries, *Living Flame of Love*, is in more ways than one the most remarkable. To write any such treatise in a fortnight is an unusual achievement, though again and again the finest of the Saint's verses and prose passages give the impression of having been composed at white heat and it is more than possible that much of his work was produced under intense strain. But such rapidity is the more amazing in a book which deals exclusively with that most ineffable of earthly experiences—"the most perfect degree of perfection to which a man may attain in this life, which is transformation in God."[22] Only, he says, because "the Lord appears to have opened knowledge somewhat to me and given

21 *Works*, I, 338.
22 *Works*, III, 16.

me some fervour,"[23] can he write of this at all. Beneath the terminology of that diffident understatement, which he had already used in writing of the *Canticle*, we can sense a period of almost superhuman insight and power of expression. It is probably true to say that no other author, either before him or since, has written of mystical Union with the unalloyed beauty which we find in this poem and its interpretation.

The four stanzas, whether composed at the same time as the commentary or previously we cannot say,[24] are themselves noteworthy. Without altering the essential nature of the *lira*, the author gives it a third rhyme and expands it into six lines—a proceeding which adds substance to it, and, in a short poem at least, makes it even more attractive. The music of the stanzas throughout is perfect—unmarred by a single harsh sound, inaccurate rhyme or halting phrase. The restrained use of alliteration, the echoing repetition of medial vowels, the melody of the feminine endings, the lavish employment of liquid consonants—all these are constituent elements of the poem's ethereal beauty. And all of them contribute to the perfection of the final line

¡Cuán delicadamente me enamoras!

where the interlacing of cunningly arranged vowels with the frailest of consonants produces one of the

[23] *Works*, III, 15.

[24] Though the language of the sub-title and the opening paragraph of the preface to the treatise (*Works*, III, 15) suggests that the poem had been written at least some little time previously.

most untranslatable musical phrases in Spanish literature.

Any poem describing the mystic's most sublime
experience—"the intimate communion of the Union
of the love of God"—must of necessity rely largely
on symbols; and it is therefore not surprising that,
taken as a whole, this should be the most highly fig-
ured poem that St. John of the Cross ever wrote. It
is, indeed, at once a series of apostrophes and a chain
of metaphors by means of which the author can refer
to experiences which no words will directly describe.
Essentially, it is an apostrophe to the Holy Spirit, in-
voked under the image of a flame which penetrates
to the depths of the soul. After begging Him (under
the same image) to consume the slender thread
which binds him to life on earth, he apostrophizes
each element of the Divine love-wounding:

> O burn that searest never!
> O wound of deep delight!
> O gentle hand! O touch of love supernal
> That quick'nest life for ever,
> Putt'st all my woes to flight,
> And, slaying, changest death to life eternal![25]

Then, as in the final stanzas of the "Spiritual Canticle," the author plunges more deeply into mystical
experience, and apostrophizes the lamps of Divine
fire—that is, the ways in which God reveals Himself
to the soul in Union—before passing to the culminating hymn of praise to God Himself:

[25] *Works*, II, 448.

How tender is the love
Thou wak'nest in my breast
When thou, alone and secretly, art there!
Whispering of things above,
Most glorious and most blest,
How delicate the love thou mak'st me bear![26]

The commentary, like that of the "Spiritual Canticle," follows the poem line by line, and like it, too, is distinguished by an extraordinary clarity, though later the author rewrote the book entirely, revising and amplifying it so that the second redaction is one-seventh as long again as the first.[27] Only once—during the exposition of the third stanza—does he digress to any extent from his sublime theme, and then it is to discourse upon a subject very present at all times to the mystics: the harm that can be done to advanced contemplatives by directors less proficient than they. Except from the standpoint of pure artistry, however, the digression is not out of place, and so pungently apposite is it that one could not desire its excision. So, evidently, the Saint also thought, for he made no attempt to modify it in his second redaction.

For the beauty of the commentary as a whole to be appreciated, it must be read straight through—and read in the spirit in which it was written. Particularly noteworthy are the expository paragraphs which paraphrase the individual stanzas and thus

[26] *Ibid.*
[27] On the genuineness of the second redaction, see *Works*, III, 6-10.

facilitate the comprehension of the entire treatise. It is true that, as the author observes, if the reader has "no experience of this, it will perhaps be somewhat obscure to him"[28]—that is, that he will fail to achieve a full realization of the nature of mystical Union. But this condition applies to a study of the records of any high adventure, whether in the physical world, the intellectual or the spiritual. It is the peculiar glory of St. John of the Cross to have brought the realms of spiritual adventure, which might have been thought impossible of encompassment, within the focus of vision of the ordinary Christian. How much of them he can distinguish, and in what detail, must depend jointly upon his determination and his spirituality.

[28] *Works*, III, 59.

CHAPTER VI

Last Days

BEFORE ST. JOHN OF THE CROSS LEFT GRANADA, in 1588, the second period of storm, which clouded the end of his life, was all but upon him. The dissensions between the Mitigation and the Reform were over, but they were succeeded by conflicts even more deplorable within the Reform itself.

To some extent these were due to the clashes of aggressive personalities—and the tragedy of such conflicts is that they often involve, not only the aggressors themselves, but others who have no desire for strife, and, like the Pauline "servant of the Lord," are "gentle unto all men, apt to teach, patient, in meekness instructing those that oppose themselves." Such a servant was John of the Cross, yet none the less the struggle between Gracián and Doria involved him in its fury.

We have already seen how Gracián had made enemies by his precocity and his habitual rashness—a defect inseparable from those qualities of energy, zeal and enthusiasm which made him so effective a leader of the Reform. The narrow majority by which he had been elected first Provincial of the Discalced was an index to the clash of opinions about him, and, once Teresa was no longer alive to give him her moral support, his reputation declined rapidly.

When, in 1585, his somewhat stormy four years' provincialate came to an end, he proposed as his successor an older man named Nicolás Doria, who was elected by twenty-six votes out of twenty-eight: it is significant, incidentally, that though Gracián and Doria were known in religion respectively as P. Jerónimo de la Madre de Dios and P. Nicolás de Jesús María, it is by their family names, contrary to Carmelite custom, that they are always called. In making the proposal, Gracián was following Teresa's exhortations that he should co-operate with Doria, but, even before her death, the two had shown signs of coming into conflict. John of the Cross, astounded at the proposal, is said to have prophesied that some day Doria would effect Gracián's expulsion from the Order—a prophecy which, shortly after the prophet's death, came true. Doria had entered the Order, from a business career, in his late thirties, and he retained the business man's essential qualities: he was a born organizer, ambitious, independent, resolute and masterful. Recognizing in Gracián a dangerous rival, he took no steps to placate him and spared him none of the consequences of his impetuosity. Within three years, Gracián had been deprived of his offices in the order—the first step to his expulsion from it.

St. John of the Cross was now Vicar-Provincial of Andalusia. For two years his work took him all over southern Spain. On February 17, 1585, he founded the convent of San José, at Málaga. On May 10, the Chapter at which Doria was elected Provincial began at Lisbon, and, on October 17, its adjourned meeting, at Pastrana. During the Christmas season of 1585, he was at Granada; in Lent 1586, at Granada, La Peñuela and Linares. On May 18, 1586, he made a new foundation at Córdoba. From Córdoba he went to Seville, whence in June he wrote that he had been superintending the installation of the Discalced nuns in a new house, and hoped, before leaving for Ecija, Málaga and Madrid, to found a friary. The last part of his plans was changed, however, by illness: twice he appears to have gone down with some kind of fever—once at Guadalcázar and once at Toledo—and the second bout forced him to miss a meeting which Doria had summoned in Madrid for August. Instead, he returned to Granada and came back, by way of Beas, Málaga and Toledo, to Madrid, bringing with him Anne of Jesus and some other sisters who were to found a new convent there. In October, he was again in the south, making a foundation at Manchuela de Jaén. December must have been an exceptionally active month, if, as it seems, he made a foundation at Caravaca, some forty-five miles west of Murcia, and also attended a meeting in Madrid. In April 1587, he was presumably at the Valladolid Chapter which reappointed him Prior at Granada; on the following Midsummer Day, he founded a house at Bujalance.

This record of physical activity is indeed a contrast

with the intense life of solitary contemplation which John had led at Monte Calvario or with the intense mental activity of the years at Los Mártires during which the majority of his commentaries were written. When one follows him in imagination over the mountainous country and considers the badness of the roads, the intense heat of the Spanish summer and the comfortless conditions under which he travelled, it is not surprising that his health faltered under the strain.

On June 19, 1588, John attended the first Discalced Chapter-General held at Madrid. A year earlier, Doria had succeeded in persuading the Pope to declare the Reform a separate Congregation, acknowledging the authority of the General of the Order but being governed in practice by a Vicar-General elected every six years by itself alone. Doria was, of course, elected the first Vicar-General, and a new method of government, which he had devised during his provincialate, came into being. This was a centralized system known as the Consulta, which set up a tribunal of seven to take over the authority formerly held by the Priors in Chapter. The system, which many felt to be at variance with the spirit of the Primitive Rule, was not established without opposition, but Doria was the type of man who readily quells opposition. Of the first consultors (*consiliarios*, as they were called) two were John of the Cross and his now aged companion, Antonio, the former Prior of Duruelo.

At the same meeting of the Chapter the headquarters of the Reformed Congregation were established at Segovia, where, on August 10, John was established as Prior of the Monastery and also as head of the Congregation during any absence of the Vicar-General. In other words, he was given primacy among the six *consiliarios* and became Doria's second-in-command.

From September 1588 to February 1589, Doria was absent on a full visitation of the Reform and John took over his responsibilities. Several of his letters written during this period show that once more he was leading a life of great intensity—an intensity expended not in writing, nor in evangelization, nor in contemplation, but in organizing and administering—which left him very little time for anything else but the occupations to which he was bound by his vows. From his letters, and for the first and last time in his life, we get the impression of a man who has more than he can do.

The messenger descended upon me at a time when I could not reply before he went on his way, and now at this moment he is waiting again.[1]

There would be a great deal to say, more than the present lack of time and the limitations of this letter allow.[2]

I am not forgetting your affairs, but it is impossible to write more now, though I have desire enough to do so.[3]

[1] *Letters*, X (*Works*, III, 277).
[2] *Ibid.*
[3] *Ibid.* (*Works*, III, 278).

Try as he would to overcome them, the demands of administration made inroads upon his spiritual life. "I am well," he says, but "my soul lags far behind."[4]

In June 1590, a chapter held at Madrid reappointed him a *consiliario*, and, apparently during Doria's further absence, he again took charge from October 1589 to May 1591. On June 1, 1591, there opened at Madrid the General Chapter which was to be the cause of his last months of suffering. He seems to have had some foreknowledge of what was to happen to him. "Father," cried one of the Segovian nuns, as he was about to set out for the capital, "perhaps Your Reverence will come back Provincial of this province!" His quiet and matter-of-fact reply, recorded independently in almost identical language by no less than five nuns, must have created a tremendous impression. "I shall be thrown into a corner like an old rag," he said.[5]

What happened at that meeting was that Doria brought to a climax his refashioning of the Reform according to his own ideas by proposing the revocation of the Teresan Constitutions of 1581. Gracián being eliminated, Doria may have thought there would be no one to protest against this. If he did, he was wrong: there was his senior *consiliario* and chief lieutenant.

---

[4] *Letters*, IX (*Works*, III, 276).

[5] The five versions of this observation, which differ only very slightly, will be found, in Spanish, in P. Bruno, p. 473.

John's protest was made and received in silence. None of his companions supported him, so complete was Doria's power. In the upshot, he was re-elected to no post or office. Presumably the Vicar-General was taking no chances and John's character must have combined with his period of authority to give him a prestige which it did not suit a dictator that any of his collaborators should possess. There was some talk of sending him to Mexico, possibly to remove him from any future list of competitors for power. The plan fell through—as probably as not because he himself made it clear that he had not the slightest desire for power. When he left the Chapter it was to be once more a simple friar.

Whatever hard words may have been said at that Chapter, and however much Doria's tyrannical inflexibility may have grated upon him, the feelings uppermost in his mind were of relief and peace. Not only, since it has been God's will, he wrote to Anne of Jesus from Madrid on July 6, 1591, "must you be glad rather than otherwise and give hearty thanks to God because things have not happened as you desired," but the change itself is not a bad one. "It is very advantageous for me, since, now that I am free and no longer have charge of souls, I can, by Divine favour, if I so desire, enjoy peace, solitude and the delectable fruit of forgetfulness of self and of all things."[6]

But the finest passage in the Saint's extant letters

[6] *Letters,* XXI (*Works,* III, 295).

—"worth a volume on Christian resignation," remarks P. Silverio, justly[7]—is preserved in the fragment of a note written on the very same day to that Segovian nun who had so gleefully depicted his return as Provincial. Such an impression did it produce upon her that she quoted from it in a deposition made a quarter of a century after receiving it. The fragment must be reproduced as it stands:

> As to my affairs, daughter, let them not trouble you, for none of them troubles me. What I greatly regret is that blame is attributed to him who has none; for these things are not done by men, but by God, Who knows what is meet for us and ordains things for our good. Think only that God ordains all. And where there is no love, put love and you will find love.[8]

At this period, John seems to have feared that he might be sent back as Prior to Segovia, where he would not only be deprived of the peace he had hoped for but would find himself embarrassingly near the centre of an administration of which he could no longer approve. One would hardly have thought there was much danger of this. The only conceivable reason that suggests itself would be the necessity of placating his hypothetical supporters; but, if none spoke in his support at the Chapter, any resentment they might have felt at his treatment would hardly have called for much alleviation, especially in the view of a rigid authoritarian like Doria.

[7] *Works*, III, 296, note.
[8] *Letters*, XXII (*Works*, III, 296). Cf. p. 118.

In any case, the step was not taken; and, at the end of July, John was sent, neither to Mexico as Provincial, nor to Segovia as Prior, but to the lonely friary of La Peñuela, as a virtual exile.

This Peñuela house had been founded in 1573, and abandoned, after three and a half years, when its community moved to Monte Calvario. But, at the request of the inhabitants of Baeza, it was re-founded on a better site eight months later.

Notwithstanding the cloud under which he came, John was well received, and, at the Prior's request, became spiritual director to the community. For the rest of his time, he was freer than he had been since the days of Monte Calvario. To an extent seldom before possible, he sought solitude with Nature and with God. Though each of the extant accounts of the various periods of his life bears testimony to the benefit which he drew from Nature, those which describe the months he spent at La Peñuela are more than ordinarily detailed. "Christ dwells in the fields," Luis de León had written; and before dawn John would be out in the country seeking Him. Sometimes he would spend whole nights at prayer in the monastery garden. Ofter he would disappear for hours at a time among the rocks. It must have been a stern test of his powers of spiritual concentration that far away were happening things which he deplored as being contrary to the very spirit of the Reform to which he had devoted his whole life. Of these happenings he was continually receiving news in letters. Yet his only extant comment upon them shows with what deep serenity he endured even this trial:

My daughter: You will already know of the many trials that we are suffering. God allows this for the glory of His elect. In silence and hope will be our strength. Commend me to God and may He make you holy.[9]

But, from the human standpoint, there were worse troubles afoot for John than a mishandling of the Reform. Evil tongues were everywhere at their work of defamation. Diego Evangelista, a member of the Consulta, was going up and down the country spreading scandal. Ugly-sounding depositions were being taken from nuns after interrogations as to John's connection with them. Whether accidentally or not, some of these statements were incorrectly copied; complaints of this were made to the Vicar-General; no notice was taken of them.[10] What was the cause of all this scandal? Had Doria been unscrupulous enough—for he was undoubtedly clever enough—to organize it? Or was it a mere whispering epidemic, devoid of real malice? Again, what was it leading to? It looked as though it would end in an attempt to deprive John of his habit. One of his most intimate disciples went so far as to prepare him for this, and, in the last in date of his letters which has come down to us, we have the Saint's resigned and placid answer:

[9] *Letters*, XXIV (*Works*, III, 297).
[10] P. Bruno, pp. 334-5.

Son, let not this grieve you, for they cannot take the habit from me save for incorrigibility or disobedience, and I am quite prepared to amend my ways in all wherein I have strayed, and to be obedient, whatsoever penance they give me.[11]

About the middle of September 1591, John fell ill. Considering the austerity of his life, and the sufferings he had undergone during his imprisonment at Toledo, his health, until his forty-fifth year, had been remarkably good. "Fever"—whatever that word may have connoted—had, so far as we know, been his only illness, and it was "fever" that attacked him again now. In the solitude of La Peñuela, no medical attention was obtainable; if he wanted treatment, he had the choice of two towns, both comparatively near at hand and some ten miles apart—Baeza, where he would have been welcomed at his own college, and Úbeda, where a Discalced foundation had quite recently been made. He chose Úbeda. "Tomorrow," he wrote, on September 21, 1591, to Doña Ana de Peñalosa, "I go to Úbeda to cure a slight bout of fever, for, as I have been suffering from it daily for over a week, I think I need medical aid, but I go with the intention of returning here again, for in truth I am deriving great good from this holy retreat."[12]

The twenty-mile journey was a trying one, for to the heat, in southern Spain often at its worst in September, was added the agony into which the jolting

[11] *Letters*, XXVI (*Works*, III, 298).
[12] *Letters*, XXV (*Works*, III, 297).

mule-back ride transformed John's already great pain. When with his companion he at length reached the monastery, he was almost dead from exhaustion. The physician found that he was suffering from neglected erysipelas in the foot. There were no comforts to be had in Discalced monasteries, and, even had there been any, John would probably not have accepted them. But, lest there should still remain trials which he had not endured, his last days on earth were marked by the intense hostility of the Úbeda Prior, whom he had had occasion to reprimand when Vicar-Provincial of Andalusia. Of this he did not fail to remind the invalid now. He seemed anxious to heap every possible indignity on him. First, he objected to the cost of the food which he required—and this he may have done before the friar who had accompanied John from La Peñuela returned there, for the Peñuela Prior, as soon as he heard of it, retaliated by sending him a supply of chickens and wheat large enough to feed a small community. Next, he forbade him visitors except by his own special permission and refused to let any of his visitors minister to him. One of the friars, however, had the excellent thought of writing to John's old friend, Antonio of Jesus, who was at that time Provincial and had treated him with great consideration when he came to La Peñuela. Fray Antonio, now turned eighty, had become, as one would expect, a rather difficult and querulous old man, but he knew John's sanctity and he was not going to permit him to be treated like this. So he came himself to Ubeda, stayed there for a week, and, before leaving, gave orders that the sick man should be thoroughly well looked after which the surly Prior dared not disobey.

Meanwhile John's "slight bout of fever" had grown worse. An operation was performed, of the rough-and-ready sort of which it is painful to-day even to hear a description, but the erysipelas gradually spread over the body and a further operation failed to relieve it. As his three months' illness wore on, it became clear that nothing could be done to save his life, and at the beginning of December the physician told him that his days were numbered.

But there was no need to tell him. With the quiet authority of sanctity, he took command of the situation, promised the friars that he would warn them of his passing, received the Viaticum, and, in full possession of his consciousness, prepared for death. One is glad to read that before it was too late the recalcitrant Prior came to his senses and received the Saint's forgiveness.

On the afternoon of December 14, 1591, John knew that his end was very near. "I shall sing Matins in Heaven," he said at one o'clock. At five: "I am happy, very happy: I shall be in Heaven to-night." Soon afterwards he was again given the Viaticum and sent his brethren away till he called them, so that for the last time he might taste the joys of communion on earth with God. At eleven, he had them summoned, and, raising himself in bed—"most serene, beautiful and happy"[13]—began to recite the *De Profundis*. The brethren made the responses and continued the commendatory prayers for the dying. Suddenly he stopped them. "Read me some verses from the *Song of Songs*," he begged. The Prior complied. Then, with a crucifix in his hands, he lay back and waited for the stroke of midnight. As the hour began to strike, "It is time for Matins," he said, and, at the first note of the bell, he died.

He was a few months short of fifty.

[13] P. Bruno (pp. 355, 482) discusses this incident, and the uncertainty as to what exactly took place in the Saint's last hours.

CHAPTER VII

Character

S O ENDED A LIFE rich in the Christian virtues but
not perhaps of outstanding interest save to students of a particular phase of religious history
During that bare half-century great men wielded
sword or quill; great rulers rose and fell; great
changes took place both in Spain and elsewhere in
Europe. The Emperor Charles abdicated in favour
of Philip the Prudent; the power of the Turks was
broken once and for all at Lepanto; the succession
of the Spanish King to the throne of Portugal gave
the Peninsula a single ruler; the designs of Spain
upon England were shattered with the Invincible
Armada. Within those fifty years occurred the whole
of the long-drawn-out meetings of the Council of
Trent; the greater part of the reigns of the three
Henries in France and of Elizabeth in England; the
births of Cervantes, Lope de Vega, Tirso de Molina,
Góngora, Quevedo, Shakespeare, Marlowe, Spenser,
Bacon, Jonson and Raleigh—of almost all the greatest men of letters, that is to say, in the greatest ages
of two countries which seemed destined to be
enemies for ever. And yet none of these events is re-
flected in the life of this humble Castilian friar, nor
does he once allude to any of them. He wielded no

sword like his precursors in letters, Garcilaso de la Vega, and in religion, St. Ignatius of Loyola. He neither celebrated the Battle of Lepanto, like Herrera, nor took part in it, like Cervantes. He could not, like St. Teresa, number among his correspondents the King's Majesty. He did not even share with his Augustinian contemporary, Luis de León, the distinction of having been arrested, imprisoned and acquitted by the Holy Inquisition—he was merely kidnapped by a bunch of officious friars and made a scapegoat for the incorrigible quarrelsomeness of his own Order.

No adventitious lustre, then, is shed upon the life of St. John of the Cross by any phase of political history. On the contrary, it is the lustre of his life and personality which immortalizes places that in other respects are humble and illumines events in themselves trivial. Who would ever have heard of Fontiveros or Duruelo had not St. John of the Cross been born in the one and begun his life-work in the other? Who would remember the name of that relentless persecutor of the Reform or of that indulgent gaoler had the prisoner been one of those friars who took a share in flogging him? What kind of man was this who could make the memories of every place and person with whom he came into contact imperishable? Let us draw nearer to him and seek his closer acquaintance.

Both in his life and in his writings, the outstanding impression he makes is that of a man of God. When still young, despite the gratitude he owes to his Medina patron, he rejects the idea of becoming a secular priest and chaplain of the hospital. He joins an Order of contemplatives, and, not content with mere retirement into the cloister, is soon planning to transfer to another which lays more stress on silence and recollection. What does this mean but that he is labouring to delve more deeply into the mysteries of solitude and striving to create for himself a life more completely hidden with Christ in God? And the success of his endeavours can be measured by the impression which he makes upon all with whom he comes into contact: not one of intellectual distinction, of organizing ability, of a magnetic personality (though these are all qualities which he possesses), but one of sheer goodness. "He was so *good* a man," reported Mother Teresa after her first long period of contact with him.[1] *Harto santo*[2]—"a real saint," as we should say in English—was her verdict after she had seen him as Confessor to the once lax but now reformed community of the Incarnation; and the word *santo*, used either as a noun or in its adjectival sense of "saintly," is continually applied to him elsewhere. "For myself, during the whole time I knew him," witnesses a friar some twenty years after his death, "I saw a simple, sincere, unaffected sanctity."[3] Mother Teresa sums up the effect which

[1] Cf. p. 32.
[2] Cf. p. 104, n. 4.
[3] *Works*, III, 346.

he produces upon others without mincing her language. "They take him for a saint," she says, "and a saint, in my opinion, he is, and has been all his life."[4]

"It always seemed that his soul was at prayer,"[5] wrote a nun who had more descriptive aptitude than most. That was as near as she could get to describing the ineffable. Just as St. John of the Cross himself sought symbols to describe the intimacy of union with God, so those who knew him had to express themselves symbolically to convey their sense of his own goodness and purity. They thought of him as a "flaming torch" and as a "white dove."[6] The torch was the apter symbol, for it typifies, not only purity, but activity and ardour: it has been taken up by a modern poet, who uses it to compare the two founders in a phrase which becomes the more striking as we think out its implications:

> Teresa, soul of fire!
> John of the Cross, spirit of ardent flame![7]

As a ruler of men the Saint is less outstanding. Not that he shows any vacillation or weakness: the young friar who was bold enough to make conditions with the revered Mother-Foundress, and, in ten years' time, was to set his face like a flint against his persecutors at Toledo would never be found hesitating or

[4] St. Teresa, *Letters*, CCIV (December 4, 1577).
[5] *Works*, III, 353.
[6] P. Bruno, pp. 306, 321-2.
[7] Antonio Machado: *Poesías completas*, Madrid, 1928, p. 209.

irresolute. But one is conscious all the time of his interior life, of his love for being unknown, of the completeness of a detachment which had become a part of his personality. When authority over others came to him, he appears to have used it well—"he had a great gift for government,"[8] it was once said of him—but that he could ever have desired authority is inconceivable. At times it fell to his lot, but it was never his vocation.

Had his life not coincided with a period of stress in his Order, this might well have been less evident. But, as things turned out, he was brought continually into the sharpest contrast with two men who, though of baser metal and on any general reckoning his inferiors, unmistakably possessed gifts, if very dissimilar ones, which belong to those intended by nature to lead men. The gifted and precocious Gracián, for all his goodness of heart and nobility of aim, was later to involve himself in sore straits through sheer unwisdom, but in the heyday of youth his charm, brilliance and fervour were magnetic. Doria, the shrewd, ruthless, prescient and calculating Italian, was as compelling in his coldness as was Gracián in his warmth: in him men felt the sheer force of naked power. Beside either of them the insignificant little friar *dont toute la gloire est à l'intérieur*[9] stood at a marked disadvantage. But then he also lived on an entirely different plane and had his

[8] *Works*, III, 336.
[9] Jacques Maritain in P. Bruno (Paris, 1929), p. 5.

own lofty and satisfying standards. If a desire came to him, he would never dream of planning—still less of intriguing—for its fulfilment: the most he would do was to express it to a friend (as he expressed his hope not to be reappointed to Baeza) and trust that it might be granted him. If he had an enemy who was determined on his downfall, he would face him fearlessly, say his say and then leave him to do his worst. His gifts as an administrator were not, like St. Teresa's, superlative (I could not call him, as one of his modern admirers does, "a virile man of affairs"),[10] but they were by no means negligible. His extant letters,[11] and the little external evidence on the subject that we possess, reveal an awareness of material needs, a considerable shrewdness and a marked sense of balance and proportion, but certainly nothing more. It is as misleading to describe him as a born organizer as to call him a man of the world. Practical, indeed, he is, but chiefly in things of the spirit. Perhaps the fairest assessment of his character would be to say that, while fully capable of doing business with this world, he was first, last and all the time a man of the next.

That being so, he naturally conceived his primary function to be the inculcation of other-worldliness, and he went about this task in the most practical way imaginable. His first essays at character-forming were similar to those of the parish priest: the evangelization of the countryside, an apostolate to the wealthy

[10] Frost, p. 8.
[11] Notably Letter IV (*Works*, III, 267-9).

and to the poor. Next, after an interval of two years divided between three houses of somewhat dissimilar kinds, he tried his hand on material that was no doubt finer than that of Duruelo, but a long way from perfection—the nuns of the Observance at Ávila. Well can we imagine how much heart-searching and agony it must have cost so skilled a workman to chisel such recalcitrant blocks of stone into images of his Master! But it was all part of his self-training, and he found his reward in the sisters of Beas. No trace of any teaching which he gave at Duruelo and Ávila has come down to us, but his labours at Beas are perpetuated in the *Ascent of Mount Carmel*, in the latter part of the "Spiritual Canticle" and its commentary, in the *Maxims*—particularly, perhaps, in the "Points of Love"—and, of course, in the few extant letters. Had not those sisters, apprehensive during the last months of his life of doing him un-witting harm, destroyed so many of his letters, it might have been possible to trace in them all the main lines of his teaching. Even in the fragments we have, written some three or four years before his death, we can recognize the authentic accents of the Doctor of the Dark Night:

He, then, that seeks pleasure in aught else keeps not himself empty that God may fill him with His ineffable joy.[12]

In order to preserve our spirituality . . . there is no better remedy than to suffer and work and be silent, and

[12] *Letters*, V (*Works*, III, 270).

to close the senses by the practice of solitude and the inclination to solitude, and forgetfulness of all creatures
and all happenings, even though the world perish.[13]

Briefly, God desires that the religious shall live the
religious life in such a way that he shall have done with
everything, and everything shall be as nothing to him.[14]

Having learned the art of training souls by long and
no doubt painful experience, the Saint's instructions
remained for the last thirteen years of his life on the
highest level. Conscious that this task was one for
which he was specially fitted, he continued to be a
specialist in the sublimest of sciences to the exclusion
of all else.

If the Saint had no great assurance or confidence
of manner with which to make a superficial impression, he created little more effect through eloquence
of speech. He seems to have been an indifferent
orator; and, partly no doubt for this reason and
partly because of his innate reserve, he never lec-
tured or taught in public and seldom even preached
sermons: the more informal any talk that he gave
could be, the better he was pleased.[15] In hearing
confessions or in directing his penitents, he loved to
speak with some spiritually-minded individual of the
soul's deepest experiences, or, at recreation or after
supper at night, he would gather around him a group

[13] *Letters*, VI (*Works*, III, 272).
[14] *Letters*, VII (*Works*, III, 273).
[15] *Works*, III, 362.

of earnest young friars or nuns and discourse to them
out of the fullness of his heart. Then they would
learn "that love was eloquence." He would draw
himself up to something like the full stature of his
greatness; his whole self would change; and he would
be transfigured before them.[16]

The testimonies of those who heard him speak in
this way are perhaps the most vivid to be found:

He spoke of spiritual things with such readiness that
one would think he had them prepared; and he needed
no material for this, but in speaking of any small thing
—even of a trifle—he would soar in his discourse so that
he carried us away with him and we listened to him
with such delight that none of us ventured to speak
until he had finished. He often spoke in this way during
recreation.[17]

His words had great efficacy and he spoke in a most
lofty manner of the love of God and of prayer and contemplation. He could speak of nothing else, and his
words were so apt that they remained in the souls of the
hearers, and enkindled in them the fire of the love of
God.[18]

I have heard it said . . . of his words, that they enkindled with celestial fire, and this I have also myself
experienced.[19]

Impressing others, then, as he did, by pure goodness shining through his every act and word, the

[16] *Ibid.*
[17] *Works*, III, 346.
[18] *Works*, III, 352-3
[19] *Works*, III, 356.

"little friar" might have been passed over in a crowd, but, once seen and spoken to alone, could never be forgotten. Perhaps his most lovable traits were "his meekness and gentleness, which were great,"[20] and his consideration for others. These he may well have developed as a boy, serving his apprenticeship to brotherly love in the Medina hospital. Of the numerous anecdotes told of him many are inspired by the narrators' evident determination to be, as it were, ahead of the Church in canonizing him; and to take literally everything that was said of him from ten to forty years after his death would be to turn him into a saint who never existed except in a church window. But many of these anecdotes, in their simplicity, their regard for detail and their agreement with other independent evidence, bear the hallmark of truth, and none of them are more consistently of this kind than those which illustrate the Saint's consideration for the sick.[21] To tempt the appetite of a sick brother, he would himself prepare and serve his meal and feed him a spoonful at a time. More, he would make his bed, nurse him like a woman and do him the most menial services.[22] All this fits in perfectly with an unassuming modesty of demeanour and a perpetual serenity which were the concomitants of his goodness.

[20] *Works*, III, 356.
[21] "He was full of charity, especially with the sick" (*Works*, III, 347.
[22] P. Bruno, p. 304.

But beneath this modest demeanour and this serenity lay one of the most resolute personalities that has ever existed. The austerity of St. John of the Cross was manifested, not in his speech or in his mien, but in his life. Save for the traces which it must certainly have left upon his features, we may be sure that his asceticism was all *à l'intérieur*: any parading of it he would have found insufferably repugnant. It should not be less so to students of his works who endeavour to catch something of his spirit. For that reason, we pass over such records as have come down to us of the punishments which he inflicted upon his body. Such forms of penance, in an age in which life of all kinds was harder than it is to-day, were taken largely as a matter of course; and the famous compact which St. Peter of Alcantara made with his body, that it should suffer on earth without intermission and after death be allowed to rest for ever, represented the ascetic's normal position. It is unnecessary, then, to doubt the accuracy of the stories told by the Saint's admirers of his self-flagellations, penitential garb and hard living: though they would lose nothing with the passage of years, they may be taken as founded upon fact. The relevant point is that they probably cost him a great deal less than some of the renunciations which to us may seem simpler. I have always thought, for example, when re-reading the letters in which St. Teresa refers to St. John of the Cross and trying to realize what the two must have been to each other,

that few things he did in his life can have been harder
than the burning of a bundle of her letters to him—
probably all he had ever had from her. But his affection for her, and his attachment to them, were coming between him and a deeper loyalty, so there was
no help for it—the letters must go.[23] That act of
detachment we may take as typical of thousands of
"little, nameless, unremembered acts," which show
us the apostle of detachment living up to his own
principles.

Yet there was nothing about St. John of the Cross
either inhuman or inhumane. The few and fleeting
glimpses which we get of his weaknesses—his dislike
of the Andalusians, his occasional bouts of loneliness,
his longing for friends, his preferences in food, and
the like—are, though comforting at times when one
tends to think of his standards as frankly unattain-
able, less revealing than the sidelights on his tastes
and attainments which help to complete the picture
given us by the main events of his life.

The Saint was anything but a narrow and warped
ascetic, a schoolman-friar with no interests beyond
his books and his cell. Student rather than craftsman
though he had shown himself to be as a child, he had
retained an interest in the crafts into which he had
achieved some insight. He drew plans, sketches and
pictures: at least one picture of Christ which he
made after experiencing a vision of Him is still in

[23] Baruzi, p. 51, n. 1; P. Bruno, p. 442, n. 130.

existence.[24] He frequently spent the leisure which
for a life of intense spiritual activity he thought as
important as food in carving crucifixes and figures.
On the religious aspect of drawing, painting and
carving he had, as we have seen, the most pronounced
opinions. Further, he would turn to any piece of
manual labour—building, painting or decorating—
that might present itself, or would even "ask for the
key of the garden and go and root up weeds and
such things; and sometimes he busied himself in
making certain walls and floors in our convent. . . .
He also liked to dress the altars, and this with great
neatness and delicacy, and in silence."[25]

But there is more to record than this. His exquisite
sensibility expressed itself in a love of music and a
passion for the beauties of Nature. Not long before
his death, when he was suffering agonies of pain, a
watcher by his bedside asked him if he might not
bring some musicians to distract his attention from
his sufferings. Three such were found, and they had
just begun to tune their guitars when the sick man
asked for them to be sent away, "for they disturbed
other and better music which he heard interiorly."[26]

If God has given me (he said) the great sufferings I
am enduring, why wish to soothe and lessen them by
music? . . . Pay them and send them away, for I wish to

[24] P. Bruno, p. 133.
[25] *Works*, III, 320.
[26] *Works*, III, 370.

endure without any relief the gracious gifts which God sends me.[27]

Now this change of mind might have been due to the strain upon the sick man's nerves caused by the tuning of the guitars, and its attribution to another cause to a desire not to give offence to the musicians. But the most important point of the testimony, which has come down to us in the words of the watcher himself, is the parenthetical explanation: "because I knew well that he had a great love for music." We may be sure that he had, for when he went on his long journeys he would beguile the time by singing as he went along.[28] Nor was music the only form of self-expression practised by this Saint who once took the bambino from the Christmas crib and danced with it in his arms out of sheer joy.[29] But there was a *música callada*, a "silent music," which he loved still more. In the "tranquillity and silence of the night," which, through long vigils, he knew so well, the sensitive soul can detect "a harmony of sublimest music surpassing all the concerts and melodies of the world." And this "silent music" is the Beloved Himself, "because this harmony of spiritual music is known and experienced in Him."[30]

But, attracted though he was by "silent music," the dominant interest of St. John of the Cross on the

[27] P. Bruno, pp. 347-8.
[28] *Works*, III, 377.
[29] P. Bruno, p. 226.
[30] *Spiritual Canticle*, XIII, XIV (*Works*, II, 88-9).

earthly plane appears to have been his love of Nature. Of this his poems alone, and his commentaries upon them, furnish sufficient proof, but it is confirmed and reinforced by external evidence, which becomes so much more definite, and abundant, as his life proceeds, that it would seem as if his love of Nature deepened with the years. At Monte Calvario, following the principles which he laid down in the *Ascent of Mount Carmel*,[31] he would take his friars, from time to time,

to a stream or pleasant rocky spot, and having spiritually entertained and recreated them . . . he divided them up and scattered them, one by one, over the mountain, to speak to God in solitude.[32]

While he was at Baeza, he was given a plot of land some five leagues from the city, and to this solitary outpost he would go with his students for as much as a week at a time, spending long periods in the meadows—and not only during the daytime, for, like Luis de León, he loved the quiet of the night and the starlit heavens.[33] At Los Mártires, he introduced and encouraged the habit of solitary meditation in the friary gardens: here he had the magnificent snow-covered mass of the Sierra Nevada almost at his doorstep, and he would continually stop to gaze at the landscape from the friary itself, or from the country around, whenever he walked there. So

[31] III, xlii (*Works*, I, 324-5).
[32] P. Bruno, p. 198.
[33] Cf. P. Crisógono, II, 80-7, *passim*.

one might go on. It was as if in his youth he had gradually come to love Nature without knowing it; when deprived of its solace had pined for it and poured out its praises in song; and when, in Andalusia, it was restored to him in fuller measure, had revelled so much in it that he could not have it to excess.

Let us end as we began: first and last, in public and in private, in what the world would call success and failure, in writing, speech and action, in his desires, preferences, accomplishments, criticisms and condemnations, St. John of the Cross was, more essentially than anything else, a man of God. In the deepest and most genuine sense, his whole life was moulded by love. "Ya sólo en amar es mi ejercicio" might have been his epitaph; and, in re-reading the "Spiritual Canticle," I often think how well the stanza which ends with these words sums up his life:

My soul has employed itself. And all my possessions in
　　his service:
Now I guard no flock nor have I now other office. For
　　now my exercise is in loving alone.[34]

The commentary on the stanza is even more illuminating. "All the ability of my soul and body is moved through love"—it reads like a personal avowal—"all that I do, I do through love, and all that I suffer, I suffer for love's sake." "Happy life and happy estate

[34] *Works*, II, 28.

and happy the soul that arrives thereat," continues the Saint, "where all is now substance of love to it."[35]

That avowal, if such it be, explains the whole of the Saint's life: he had brought the practice of love to well-nigh the highest degree of perfection imaginable. And it was love which inspired him, not only with those traits which the world approves, or at least finds comprehensible—such as thoughtfulness, gentleness, care for the weak and sickly—but with others which are apt to arouse polite incredulity. But St. John of the Cross really did prefer being a simple friar to holding high office. He really did wish to suffer before he died. He really did desire to die where he was not even known.

It is said that letters to friends are more revelatory even than the most intimate of conversations—that the act of writing is less conducive to that unconscious pose and affectation from which few are entirely free than the act of speech. Certainly in that extant handful of letters which St. John of the Cross wrote to his sons and daughters in Christ we have a more nearly complete self-revelation than in all the eulogies made of him after his death. More than anywhere else, we seem to hear the man himself speaking. And nowhere does he give us the key to his character better than in a simple phrase from a fragment, already once quoted, of a letter written when he was in the deep waters of trial:

[35] *Works*, II, 113.

... And where there is no love, put love in and you will draw love out.[36]

The recipe must rank with the Wise Man's dictum on the soft answer as one of the simplest yet profoundest things ever said upon the art of human relations. It will be a long time before anyone says anything better.

[36] *Works*, III. 296, Cf. p. 94. The last verb is *sacar*, which means literally to take out or draw out. The translation here given is therefore more literal, though less polished, than that on p. 94.

PART II

The Mystic and the World of To-day

CHAPTER I

Uniqueness of St. John of the Cross

IN HIS BRILLIANT if occasionally slightly erratic study of St. John of the Cross as a mystical writer, the Carmelite scholar P. Crisógono makes bold to term him, in the most literal sense of the word, *unique*.[1]

This is hardly, if at all, an exaggeration. It is customary, in writing of the Spanish mystics, to place him on a pedestal by the side of St. Teresa, a practice justified by the immense superiority of either of the two over any other of their contemporaries. But while St. Teresa, as has been said, was one of the most remarkable women who have ever lived, and while her mystical writings not only touch great heights, but, by reason of her extraordinary personal qualities, make an unusually wide appeal to all types of Christian, she cannot, in my view, as a pure mystic, and if judged by the whole body of her work, be compared with St. John of the Cross. She continually delights the reader, and sometimes, now by her versatile and flexible mind, now by her sheer power, surprises him. But she has not the scientific bend of her "little Seneca." Her knowledge of the human

[1] P. Crisógono, I, 63: "Con tales condiciones el catolicismo no tiene más que un místico: san Juan de la Cruz."

heart, for all its intimacy, derives from her native shrewdness and from the unerring instinct of sanctity —not, like his, from study as well. She has not the advantage of his wealth of reading, of his gifts for generalization or of his command of argument. She knows more of theology than can have seemed natural, or even proper, to the simple nuns who flocked to her foundations; but she was not, like Father John, a theologian. Nor has she his grasp of the contemplative life as a whole; she could plan and write a "little book," but she could never have constructed a system. The entire corpus of her work, replete as it is with digressions, repetitions and reminiscences, might be described as what the *Book of her Life* sets out to be—an immense and comprehensive spiritual autobiography, written in the main for the devout but unlearned. The writings of St. John of the Cross, on the other hand, form nothing less than a contemplative's library, and a library stocked with works of such profoundity and fullness that few readers, even if trained for their task, could hope to assimilate it in a lifetime.

So far as my own reading goes, in fact, St. John of the Cross, considered as a mystic, has only two rivals in the whole history of Christian literature. One of these is St. Augustine, whom I whole-heartedly join with Abbot Butler in terming "Prince of Mystics,"[2] for in his own field he can have no rival. His descriptions of mystical experience have neither the detail

---

[2] *Western Mysticism*, London, 1922, p. 24.

nor the richness of the Carmelite Doctor's, but for power, intensity and spiritual insight he is unparalleled. Outside the Scriptures, indeed, I know no writer in any language who can inspire awe and reverence—who can almost strike one down in the way that the young man Saul was struck down by the heavenly vision—as can the author of the superb mystical passages in the seventh, nine and tenth books of the *Confessions*. The other is the fourteenth-century Fleming Blessed John Ruysbroeck, whose mystical works, though well known, are all too little read, and whose sublimest pages—for the most part those in which he writes of the ineffable experiences of the Life of Union—can hardly be surpassed for dazzling and penetrating beauty. But with the ethereal quality of much of his work goes a disconcerting vagueness as far removed from the precision of the Castilian Carmelite as are the northern mists from the translucent atmosphere of the south, and his presentation of the mystical life as a whole lacks St. John's cogency of completeness.

Of all the remaining Christian mystics, from sub-apostolic times down to the present day, it is doubtful if a single one can fairly be called his equal. Many have written distinctively, and with distinction, upon individual phases of the contemplative life, but of none that I know can the writings as a whole be compared with his, nor is there one but lacks something which we find in him. For centuries, even in his own Spain, he has been passed over or misinterpreted by all save the few; between 1703, when the first spate of editions of his treatises subsided, and 1912, the date of the first modern critical edition ever to be made, his works were hardly re-published at all. Fifty years ago, the tercentenary of his death evoked but the slightest notice, and only with the new century did men begin once more to appreciate his greatness. But if his light has lain for too long under a bushel, it has at last been set on a candlestick and its steady flame is penetrating to every corner of the house.

What are the features in St. John's presentation of the Mystic Way that have combined to give it this character of uniqueness? Taking them broadly, it would seem that there are three.

First, it has spatial and architectural qualities which can be summarized under the headings of *unity, range and method*. It is a striking reflection that critics and panegyrists have in turn associated St. John of the Cross, more or less exclusively, with every one of the principal elements of his teaching. Thus his frequent use of such phrases as "Desire to possess nothing,"[3] "Blessed is that nothingness,"[4] has gained him the title of *Doctor de la Nada* (Doctor of Nothingness), as though his doctrine were entirely negative. But if those sentences are completed, so that they read:

[3] *Ascent*, I, xiii (*Works*, I, 63).
[4] *Letters*, XV (*Works*, III, 286).

> In order to arrive at possessing everything
> Desire to possess nothing,

and

> Blessed is that nothingness and blessed is that secret place of the heart that is of such great price that it possesses everything,

it will be seen that a more appropriate title—and what a magnificent, triumphant title it is!—would be *Doctor del Todo*: Doctor of the All.

In the past, again, critics have dwelt exclusively upon his expositions of the Dark Night: the conscientious if unsympathetic and ill-documented Inge, following the positively hostile and no better informed Vaughan, mentions none of his works but the *Ascent of Mount Carmel* and the *Dark Night of the Soul*. And this is no mere Protestant prejudice, for to the average Spaniard who knows anything about such matters St. John of the Cross is the "Doctor of the Dark Night" *tout court*. P. Crisógono, writing in Spanish for Spanish readers, has to protest against the "vulgar notion" that the Saint's originality is all connected with the "nights of the soul."[5] Others go to the contrary extreme, describe the "principal and central point of his entire doctrine" as "transforming union" and his works as "much more a treatise on union than a treatise on contemplation,"[6] and thus make him, in effect, the Doctor of

[5] P. Crisógono, I, 303.
[6] Fr. Gabriel de Ste-Marie-Madeleine, O.C.D.: "L'union transformante," in *Saint Jean de la Croix* ("Extrait de la *Vie Spirituelle*"), mai (1927), pp. 85, 87.

the Living Flame. Others, again, struck (as well they may be) by his maxims and counsels on love, see him, first and foremost, as the Doctor of Divine Love. He is all these, and more. No title, then, can be more appropriate than that conferred on him in 1926, on the second centenary of his canonization, by Pius XI: "Doctor of the Church Universal."

For he does in fact make a universal appeal, and perhaps the most remarkable thing about his work, with the possible exception of its profundity, is its combination of unity with extensiveness of range. He plunges into the abyss of purgation; describes with the unerring precision of the skilled director the enthusiasm and the imperfections of the newly awakened soul; and passes on to a description of the Night of Sense, the realism of which might be thought unsurpassable until it is compared with the literally terrifying realism of the Night of the Spirit. Characteristic, too, of his treatment of the Second Night is its subtlety: books have been written upon it and learned men have disagreed as to its exact nature. Stygian in its blackness beside the "Divine darkness" of contemplation which St. John of the Cross takes over from the pseudo-Dionysius, the Second Night is easily enough distinguished from the first,[7] but the description of it as "an inflowing of God into the soul . . . called by contemplatives infused contemplation, or mystical theology,"[8] and

[7] *Dark Night*, I, viii (*Works*, I, 371).
[8] *Op. cit.*, II, v (*Works*, I, 405).

the elaboration of its positive and negative (or active and passive) aspects makes it a fit subject for long and careful study. To have gone through, and survived, the experiences of the two Nights and then to have penned such precise and full descriptions of them might well be the work of a lifetime. And yet, besides having left what will always be classical pages on subjects more or less closely connected with the Dark Night—such as detachment, aridity, quiet, meditation contrasted with contemplation, visions and locutions—not to mention such purely ascetic themes as the evils of desire, the qualities of an efficient director, or the imperfections of beginners contrasted with those of proficients, he has also soared to heights reached by very few and led us farther than might have been thought possible—perhaps than, before beginning to write, he himself thought possible—into the life of Union. Nor are his descriptions of Union mere spiritual *reportage* or autobiography metaphorically and objectively presented. Partly, no doubt, because both experiences transcend description and partly because of his own intellectual stature, his teaching on the Spiritual Marriage is as subtle as his teaching on the Spiritual Night.

In describing the three poems which served St. John of the Cross as texts for his four commentaries we observed how some of them dealt by implication, and as exclusively as is possible in poetry, with certain aspects of the mystical life, and some with certain others. If these poems could be combined into one artistic whole, no part of that life would be left uncovered. The commentaries, however, can and should be considered as one whole, for that is precisely what they are intended to be. The mystical life, and for that matter the pre-mystical or ascetic life, of which a great deal is said in the four treatises, is, like physical life, one continuous process. Even the stages into which, for convenience of treatment, it is traditionally mapped out are not mutually exclusive. Some element in one will impinge upon another, or even overwhelm it. The traveller in the valley of Quiet will suddenly be plunged into the Dark Night of Sense; the austerities of the Purgative Way will be lightened by gleams of authentic Illumination; and so on. As a later Spanish mystic put it, we cannot distinguish "three Ways, one following the other, so that a soul cannot pass to the last without having been for definite periods of time in the first two."[9] St. John of the Cross is particularly realistic here, which is probably the reason why many of his commentators have disagreed about his presentation of the *via mystica*.[10] Further, he is not content, as some of his lesser Spanish contemporaries are, to throw into relief any single experience at the expense of others. He has mapped out the whole Way and he entreats the reader who would understand him to read him as a whole:

[9] Juan Falconi. Cf. *Studies*, II, 371.
[10] For a suggestive treatment of this subject, see "The Three Ways," in Frost, pp. 399-406.

Let not the reader marvel if it seem to him somewhat dark also. This, I believe, will be so at the beginning when he begins to read; but, as he passes on, he will find himself understanding the first part better, since one part will explain another.[11]

And this assurance is fully justified. While it is true that his theme, at its greatest heights, is such that only those with an experience comparable to his own can wholly comprehend it, it is undeniable that he treats it with the greatest possible degree of clarity. So logical and so clear is his exposition as to be almost deceptive. It is sometimes maintained that the mystics should only be read by professed contemplatives, because the superficial and uninstructed reader is apt to be led into the unconscious presumption of supposing his rudimentary religious experiences to be like theirs. The danger is a real one, though I believe the risk is worth taking. And, strange as it may seem, there is no mystic more liable to be misinterpreted in this way than St. John of the Cross. The uninitiated are sometimes tempted to think that the Way must be easy, just because of the precision with which he explains to them how and why it is hard.

A second outstanding characteristic of these works is *the intense and evident subjectivity underlying their marked objectivity of form.* Except in his letters the Saint rarely uses the pronoun "I," and, when he

[11] *Works,* I, 14-15.

does so, he is nearly always referring to some comparatively trivial matter, as in the chapter of the *Dark Night of the Soul* I, iii) which discusses attachment to objects of devotion. Here his sudden excursion into reminiscence, quite Teresan in type, comes almost as a shock:

> For true devotion must issue from the heart, and consists in the truth and substance alone of what is represented by spiritual things; all the rest is affection and attachment proceeding from imperfection; and in order that one may pass to any kind of perfection it is necessary for such desires to be killed.
> I knew a person who for more than ten years made use of a cross roughly formed from a branch that had been blessed, fastened with a pin twisted round it; he had never ceased using it, and he always carried it about with him until I took it from him. . . .[12]

In this apparent objectivity St. John of the Cross contrasts markedly with many mystical writers— foremost among them St. Teresa—who are continually illustrating their teaching by references to their own experiences and even disgressing for pages on end into autobiography. Superficially, there is hardly more subjectivity in St. John of the Cross than in the Spaniards of the seventeenth century whose writings on mystical theology are mere codifications of those of their predecessors. And yet there is no mystic who more unmistakably conveys the impression of consistently writing from personal experience, which he describes as an essential part of mystical theology

[12] *Works*, I, 357.

—the "science of love."[13] Just as some of his lesser
contemporaries display their erudition by making
frequent long quotations from the best authorities,
whereas he himself had assimilated his learning so
completely that in order to find his sources, other
than the Bible, we have to search for them, so, while
others talk openly and freely of their spiritual experiences, he prefers to translate what he has seen, heard,
felt and learned into an apparently objective form.

But it would be a very insensitive reader who
failed to realize that the Saint is writing, not of what
he has gathered from books, but of what he has himself experienced. He teaches truths which he knows
and he knows the truth of what he teaches. In those
wonderful passages of the *Ascent of Mount Carmel*
which discuss the psychology of desire and mortification we hear the authentic and unmistakable voice
of the director and confessor. In the terribly realistic
descriptions of the Second Night in the *Dark Night
of the Soul* we are listening to the personal witness
of a solitary contemplative. In the *Living Flame of
Love*, instinct in places as it is, and almost trembling,
with emotion, we are listening to one who has
emerged from "those secret haunts divine," the soul's
innermost mansions, and is ransacking his imagination to find symbols by which he can represent what
he has experienced there.

Anyone who has the least doubt about this will
find ample proof in the prefaces to the works in

[13] *Spiritual Canticle,* Prologue *(Works,* II, 25). Cf. p. 151.

question. In the *Ascent*, he says that, "in order to expound and describe this dark night . . . it would be necessary to have illumination of knowledge *and experience* other and far greater than mine;"[14] adds that "only he that passes this way can understand it;" and promises that, though trusting "neither to experience nor to knowledge," since these "may fail and deceive," he will make use of both.[15] The stanzas expounded in the *Spiritual Canticle* were composed "under the influence of a love which comes from abounding mystical knowledge"[16] — experiential knowledge, that is to say, for "no words of holy doctors, despite all that they have said and may yet say, can ever expound these things fully."[17] The undertaking, similar to that given in the *Ascent*,[18] "not to affirm aught that is mine, trusting to my own experience or to that of other spiritual persons," save when it is confirmed by Scripture, implies that such experience will in fact be used: indeed, the Saint goes on to say: "I purpose to profit by both."[19] In the *Living Flame*, he points out that "it is hard to speak of that which passes in the depths of the spirit if one have not deep spirituality," and continues:

Now that the Lord appears to have opened knowledge somewhat to me and given me some fervour . . . I have

14 *Works*, I, 11. Italics mine.
15 *Ibid.*
16 *Works*, II, 24.
17 *Ibid.*
18 Cf. p. 178.
19 *Works*, II, 25.

taken courage, knowing for certain that of my own power I can say naught that is of any value, especially in things of such sublimity and substance.[20]

As one lives with the Saint, however, and becomes able, in some small degree, to enter into his mind, these assurances are needed less and less. There are other signs that one is writing of one's own experiences than the use of the first personal pronoun.

Thirdly, St. John of the Cross is unique among mystics in the *variety of his attainments*. His saintliness, his powerful intellect, his keen perception and his wide reading all contribute to his expositions, at once experiential and doctrinal, of mystical theology. An expert psychologist, he has not learned all his psychology in books. He knows his philosophy, and, of course, his scholastic theology: many critics believe, too, that he assimilated more than a few of the mediaeval mystics. He is a man of the world, precisely because he lives apart from the world, and his familiarity with human nature is accompanied by an understanding of it given only to those who can regard it with complete objectivity. Finally—and this is not the least remarkable of his attainments— he is essentially, in his prose as well as in his verse, a poet.

A full justification and development of these assertions would necessitate a comprehensive study of St. John of the Cross's teaching; and, as there exist several such studies, some of quite recent date, I

[20] *Works*, III, 15-16.

have no intention of attempting another. Let it suffice to describe the impression of variety which his work produces in the words of an erudite and sensitive student of to-day.

St. John of the Cross gives us everything. He is philosopher and poet, theologian and man of letters, a mystic in experience and in his doctrine. Sometimes, as in the *Dark Night*, his work is grim and swathed in deep shadow; sometimes gay and colourful, as in the *Spiritual Canticle*, the pages of which have all the brightness and fragrance of spring. Sometimes he adheres closely to the method of the Schools; and then he is inflexibly logical, his tones are those of a master and he resembles a dictator as he lays down the law. He is like this in the *Ascent of Mount Carmel*. But there are times when he moves with greater freedom, breaks through the rigid forms of an idiom incapable of expressing the loftiest mystical conceptions and soars on wings of genius to the highest regions of mystical philosophy, enshrining his thoughts in a magnificent and sublime language of his own creation. He is like this in many of the pages of the *Living Flame*.[21]

[21] P. Crisógono, I, 71-2.

CHAPTER II

The Poets' Poet

WHILE THE WHOLE OF THESE CLAIMS can be sub-
stantiated by the student who reads only English, the pre-eminence of St. John of the Cross as a
poet cannot be fully appreciated save by those who
study him in the original. His mingling of theology
and philosophy with poetry is a characteristic which
no other mystic possesses in the same degree. Though
the mere initial contact with his major poems
suffices to indicate his greatness, a more intensive
study will bring out "new glories," which are largely
responsible for the satisfaction that he gives to all
lovers of poetry.

The Authorized Version of the Bible, by God's
providence, was planned in an epoch when English
prose was at its best; it was at a like fullness of time
that St. John of the Cross embraced the vocation of
poetry. Only at the beginning of this twentieth century has the Spanish lyric genius approached the
heights to which it rose in the sixteenth. Had this
poet been born in a mediaeval Spain still struggling
for lyrical expression, in the *barroco* days of the late
Golden Age, in the barrenness of the eighteenth century or in the gilt and tinsel world of a Hugoesque
or neo-mediaeval romanticism, his verses would have

captivated fewer than his prose would have edified. As it was, he came into a literary world in which the original genius of Spain was newly wedded to the art of Italy, and, as both his own words[1] and his poems themselves tell us, he was as fully alive as his great predecessors, Boscán and Garcilaso de la Vega, to the charm of those "lascivious metres" of the Italian Renaissance.[2] But our great cause for satisfaction must be that he caught the poetical language of Spain, as it were, at a moment when with richness of conception and a capacity for imaginative and emotional flight—even for sustained flight—it combined simplicity, dignity and restraint. And those characteristics of his age are synthetized and carried to a most intense degree in his own poetry. He was, I believe, a supremely skilful artist endowed in the highest measure with natural ability. It is by no mere chance that those epithets of his—notably in the "Spiritual Canticle"—are so perfect in themselves and yield so much to the imagination. Either his stanzas were kneaded, pulled to pieces and refashioned again and again in the cell of his mind— "polished and repolished ceaselessly" as the French preceptist has it—or he was possessed of the most marvellously intuitive poetic faculty imaginable and developed what the Catalan Maragall was later to call the art of the "living word" (*paraula viva*) to an extent heretofore unknown. To me the former hy-

[1] Cf. p. 64, n.
[2] Cf. R. L., pp. 69-70.

pothesis seems by far the more credible and fully borne out by such admittedly slender external evidence as we have.

Nor was it only in his three mystical poems, each of which has been referred to in turn, that St. John of the Cross reached a high level of art and emotion. I have just praised the poem "Although 'tis night," the beauty of which has also been commented upon by one of the foremost Spanish poets living.[3] Elsewhere[4] I have mentioned the lovely little pastoral allegory of the shepherd-boy who becomes a martyr to his love, which trembles with a latent emotion quite absent from the type of poem to which it technically belongs. Less successful, perhaps, but by no means without charm and power, are the poet's treatments of those well-known stanzas from the *Cancioneros* which make conventional play with paradox and hyperbole and which he serenely glosses *a lo divino*. Such are:

> I enter'd in—I knew not where—
> And, there remaining, knew no more,
> Transcending far all human lore.[5]

> I live, yet no true life I know,
> And, living thus expectantly,
> I die because I do not die.[6]

> To win love's chase, I took my way,
> And, full of hope, began to fly.

[3] Cf. p. 138.
[4] R. L., pp. 26-7 (*Works*, II, 453).
[5] *Works*, II, 448-50.
[6] *Works*, II, 450-1.

I soar'd aloft and soar'd so high
That in the end I reach'd my prey.[7]

Yet it is of course by his three greatest poems that he will live: an extraordinary achievement, when one comes to think of it—to jump, not merely into the literary history of one's country, but into the very highest rank of European poets, by means of a handful of just over fifty stanzas. And it may be worth while pointing out that he is not only a poet, but a poet's poet, whom, in these days of a Spanish lyrical renaissance, contemporary singers revere as perhaps no other. The apostrophe addressed to him by Antonio Machado, whose indebtedness to his inspiration is evident, has already been quoted. Juan Ramón Jiménez, the spiritual father of nearly all contemporary Spanish poets, one of whose early collections, *La Soledad sonora*, was named after a line of the "Spiritual Canticle," recently remarked, concerning three lines from "Although 'tis night":

Its origin I know not—it has none. . . .

I know that naught beside can be so fair. . . .

Well know I that its depths can no man plumb. . . .[8]

"I do not believe it is possible to give a better definition of poetry than those three lines, for which no praise is excessive."[9] His contemporary, Pedro

[7] *Works*, II, 452.
[8] *Works*, II, 454.
[9] "Poesía y literatura." In *University of Miami Hispanic-American Studies*, 1941, II, 83.

Salinas, one of the foremost and most genuinely inspired of modern poets, says of the Saint's half-dozen greatest poems: "Each one of them is an extremely intense condensation, a highly powerful extract, of all the poetic intuitions of the author. They give an impression of being charged with poetic potency *like no other work written in this world.*"[10] And these quotations could easily be multiplied.

But St. John of the Cross is also a poet in his prose, and the very abundance of his talent in this respect throws into sharper relief the austerity of his doctrine. The sum total of his merits as a writer of prose, of which its poetical quality is of course only one, constitutes a very remarkable achievement; for, although when he began his treatises Spanish prose had climbed a considerable distance towards the summit which it was to reach by the beginning of the next century, the outstanding religious writers had been, and continued to be, almost exclusively ascetic. There had, in fact, been very little mystical prose at all, and that little had mainly been concerned with one aspect of mystical experience—the Prayer of Quiet.[11] St. John of the Cross had therefore to invent phrases in order to express ideas which previously had had no outlet in Spanish,[12] and his originality in this respect is not sufficiently appreci-

[10] *Reality and the Poet in Spanish Poetry*, Baltimore, 1940, p. 120. Italics mine.
[11] *Stud:es*, I, 101-11, 156-62; II, 47-76, *passim.*
[12] P. Crisógono, II, 131-2.

ated, since they were so frequently used by writers who followed him. I have drawn attention elsewhere to the number and variety of his images, and it would be easy, did space permit, to enlarge upon the skill and the facility with which he uses them.[13] Another outstanding feature of his prose is its freedom from the superabundance of proper names and the long, dreary quotations with which his contemporaries interlard their treatsies. His language is admittedly that of a *letrado*, and he is less easily understanded of the people than St. Teresa, who, as P. Crisógono admirably puts it, is "simple"—that is to say, free from ornament and flights of eloquence—whereas he is "natural"—that is to say, free from affectation.[14] But within the limits which a scholar may fairly allow himself, his vocabulary is uncomplicated by tricks and habits and as "pure" (*castizo*) as that of any of his contemporaries.

Undoubtedly his prose is marred by inequalities. Not one of the four treatises, for example, is free from passages full of long, loosely-built sentences or awkward parentheses. But a more striking and characteristic inequality, which is no defect, but a merit, and even a glory of his prose, is the variety of style and tone to be found in the different treatises. The *Ascent of Mount Carmel* fluctuates between a pleasant, familiar discursiveness and the almost staccato brevity of the *Maxims*; its emotional tone re-

---

[13] Cf. *Works*, III, 455-8.
[14] P. Crisógono, II, 141-2.

mains on a level seldom disturbed by eloquence. In the *Dark Night of the Soul* images are more numerous, discursiveness predominates, and there is a larger proportion of lengthy and formless periods; yet, strange to say, one gets the impression of a maturer mind. This may be due in part to its deeper note of personal experience and to a gravity which befits the solemnity of the theme the author is describing. The *Spiritual Canticle* has some of the author's most brilliant passages: its language is picturesque and highly adorned with figures of speech; its tone, always happy and serene, often suggests a positively care-free and light-hearted saintliness, which, to me at least, recalls the author's sojourns at Beas. At the same time its prose is correct and its style has the minimum of inequality. The *Living Flame of Love* has a few almost pedestrian pages reminiscent of the *Ascent*, but in general is ecstatic and ardent in tone, and in style eloquent and highly rhythmical: one can well believe that it was written at white heat, in a short space of time, whereas the *Canticle* was composed little by little and subjected to careful revision.

This leads us naturally to the poetic quality in St. John of the Cross's prose. Lyric emotion in the four treatises takes two forms. In the *Spiritual Canticle* it is latent in the imagery and is continually rising to the surface. In the *Living Flame* it expresses itself in frequent outbursts of great force and eloquence. In the *Ascent* and the *Dark Night* it hardly exists—there is only sober prose.

It is remarkable that the poetry of the "Canticle" should be intensified, rather than destroyed, in a theological commentary. "Do not all charms fly," the poet Keats once asked,

> At the mere touch of cold philosophy?[15]

Not when the philosopher happens also to be a poet, is the answer. The beautiful lines:

> Mi Amado las montañas,
> Los valles solitarios nemorosos. . . .
>
> My love is as the hills,
> The lonely valleys clad with forest-trees. . . .[16]

more sonorous though they are in the original than in any translation, do not surpass the grave but moving passage which glosses them, with its fleeting suggestions of assonance and rhyme, its effective parallelisms and its perfect balance and rhythm:

> Las montañas tienen alturas, son abundantes, anchas, hermosas, graciosas, floridas y olorosas. Estas montañas es mi Amado para mí. . . .
>
> Los valles solitarios son quietos, amenos, frescos, umbrosos, de dulces aguas llenos. . . . Estos valles es mi Amado para mí. . . .
>
> The mountains have heights: they are abundant, extensive, beautiful, graceful, flowery and fragrant. These mountains my Beloved is to me. . . .

15 *Lamia*, Part. II.
16 *Works*, II, 444.

The solitary valleys are quiet, pleasant, cool, shady, abounding in fresh water. . . . These valleys my Beloved is to me. . . .[17]

The phrase

> La noche sosegada
> En par de los levantes de la Aurora,

(translated as literally as the Spanish permits: "The tranquil night, at the time of the rising dawn"[18] is far less evocative than the sensitive development of it in the commentary which contrasts the "dark night" with "the night which is already near the rising of the morning."[19] In the commentary on the following stanza the Biblical phrase "our flowery bed" blossoms anew as the soul sees in itself

the flowers of the mountains whereof we spoke above, which are the abundance and greatness and beauty of God; . . . the lilies of the wooded valleys . . . ; the fragrant roses of the strange islands . . . ; the water-lilies from the sounding rivers . . . ; and intertwined and enlaced with these . . . the delicate scent of the jasmine. . . .[20]

And not only numerous passages like these but others abounding in imaginative and even daring comparisons enhance the poetic quality of this remarkable commentary. Such are the likening of spiritual aridity to "the coolness of winter morn-

---

[17] *Works*, II, 77-8.
[18] *Works*, II, 87. The plural form, *levantes*, has no exact equivalent in English.
[19] *Ibid.*
[20] *Works*, II, 93. The passage should be read in its entirety.

ings;"[21] of the Christian virtues to the kernels of a pine-cone;[22] of the "digressions of the imagination" to "birds of swift wing, since they are light and subtle in their flight first to one place and then to another."[23] In short, even to the reader looking for poetry rather than for spiritual instruction, the commentary will be found as fruitful as the poem on which it is fashioned.

For an adequate appreciation of the eloquence of the *Living Flame of Love*, more chapters would be necessary than we can spare pages. "Far hence," the Saint had cried, "be the rhetoric of the world; far hence the loquacity and arid eloquence of weak and ingenious human wisdom, wherein Thou hast no pleasure; and let us speak words to the heart."[24] But even as he speaks words to the heart, his own heart overflows, and on page after page of this swiftly written treatise his emotion seems almost to pass beyond his control. Hence the fervid ejaculations and apostrophes which go far towards making the whole book a poem in prose. Some of these are directed to persons who have not the desire or the determination that he would wish for them:

Oh, the great glory of you souls that are worthy to attain to this supreme fire, which, while it has infinite power to consume and annihilate you, consumes you

21 *Works*, II, 118.
22 *Works*, II, 132.
23 *Works*, II, 146.
24 "Spiritual sentences and maxims," Prologue (*Works*, III, 240).

not, but will grant you a boundless consummation in glory. . . .[25]

Oh, souls that seek to walk in security and comfort! If ye did but know how necessary it is to suffer and endure in order to reach this lofty state, and of what great benefit it is to suffer and be mortified in order to reach such lofty blessings, ye would in no way seek consolation, either from God or from the creatures, but would rather bear the cross . . . ![26]

Oh, how happy is this soul that is ever conscious of God reposing and resting within its breast![27]

But more characteristic, perhaps, are the pure apostrophes inspired by the lines

> O wound of deep delight!
> O gentle hand! O touch of love . . . ![28]

In these, while still maintaining the rhythm and balance of his prose, he makes use of paradox and hyperbole, and of the devices of parallelism, repetition and even (in the Spanish) alliteration, with an art which hides art and gives the impression of sweet yet impassioned melody. Such a passage as the following deserves careful study, both for the perfection of its rhythm and for the profusion of liquids and palatals. No translation will reproduce the fullness of its verbal beauty:

[25] *Works*, III, 42.
[26] *Works*, III, 52-3.
[27] *Works*, III, 112.
[28] *Works*, II, 448.

¡Oh dichosa llaga, hecha por quien no sabe sino sanar!
¡Oh venturosa y muy dichosa llaga, pues no fuiste hecha
sino para regalo y deleite del alma! Grande es la llaga,
porque grande es el que la hizo; y grande es su regalo,
pues el fuego de amor es infinito, y se mide según su
capacidad.

Oh, happy wound, inflicted by One Who can do
naught else than heal! Oh, fortunate and most happy
wound, for thou wert inflicted only for the relief and
delight of the soul! Great is the wound, since great is He
that has inflicted it; and great is its relief, since the fire
of love is infinite and is measured according to its
capacity.[29]

In later passages ("Oh, hand . . . !," "Oh, delicate
touch . . . !,") while maintaining the standard of
his technique, the poet becomes more subtly personal
and therefore more deeply moving. The alliteration
of dentals suggested by the words *toque delicado* is
perhaps almost too noticeable:

¡Oh, pues, tú, toque delicado, Verbo Hijo de Dios,
que por la delicadez de tu ser divino penetras sutilmente
la sustancia de mi alma, y tocándola toda delicadamente
la absorbes toda a ti . . . !

Oh, delicate touch, Thou Word, Son of God, Who,
through the delicateness of Thy Divine Being, dost
subtly penetrate the substance of my soul, and, touching
it wholly and delicately, dost absorb it wholly in Thyself . . . ![30]

[29] *Works*, III, 43. This and the following Spanish orginals are
taken from P. Silverio, IV, 31, 36.
[30] *Works*, III, 47.

But emotion then conquers art; and, to one critic's ear at least, the repetitions grow clumsy and the phrases lose their balance, as the poet pours forth his deepest feelings:

¡Oh aire delgado!; como eres aire delgado y delicado, di: ¿cómo tocas delgada y delicadamente siendo tan terrible y poderoso? ¡Oh dichosa, y muy dichosa, el alma a quien tocares delgadamente, siendo tan terrible y poderoso! Dilo al mundo. Mas no lo digas al mundo, porque no sabe de aire delgado el mundo, y no te sentirá, porque no te puede recibir ni te puede ver.

Oh, gentle air, that are so delicate and gentle! Say, how dost Thou touch the soul so gently and delicately when Thou art so terrible and powerful? Oh, blessed, thrice blessed, the soul whom Thou dost touch so gently though Thou art so terrible and powerful! Tell it out to the world! Nay, tell it not to the world, for the world knows naught of air so gentle, and will not hear Thee, because it can neither receive Thee nor see Thee.[31]

So, even in the prose of St. John of the Cross, feeling and art strive together for the mastery. Never, surely, has there been a mystic who with his great gifts of the spirit has combined such a gift of song.

[31] *Works*, III, 48.

CHAPTER III

The Mystics' Mystic

PRE-EMINENT THOUGH HE WAS AS A POET—and as mystic, ascetic and religious reformer—it is his life and his mystical writings which give him the firmest assurance of immortality. No treatment of him which lays the main stress on anything but his personal saintliness and the heights of communion with God to which he attained and pointed others can be considered as more than partial. Just as in Spain he is the poets' poet, so to the whole of Christendom he is, and will always be, the mystics' mystic. No contemplative, however advanced, will fail to have recourse to him, and to find in him enlightenment and inspiration. He has journeyed farther than most; he is beneath the level of none; and yet he possesses the great gift of being intelligible to all.

One can go beyond this and recall that it is for mystics and would-be mystics that his commentaries are primarily written—a fact which he is quick to point out to those about to read him. "Nor is my principal intent to address all," he says in the preface to the *Ascent of Mount Carmel*, "but rather certain persons . . . who . . . are already detached from

the temporal things of this world."[1] "Before we
enter upon the exposition of these stanzas," remarks
the preface to the *Dark Night of the Soul*, "it is well
to understand here that the soul that utters them is
now in the state of perfection."[2] The *Spiritual Canticle* concerns those who, "by the favour of God,
have left behind the beginners' state," for "there are
so many things written for beginners."[3] The *Living
Flame*, though addressed to a woman living in the
world, deals not only with "high and rare favours,"
but (the hyperbole is pardonable in one seeking to
express the ineffable) with "a love which is even
more complete and perfected" than that of the
Spiritual Canticle, though this describes "the most
perfect degree of perfection to which a man may
attain in this life."[4] The *Living Flame*, therefore,
must be even more particularly intended for proficients.

At the same time, even were the Saint writing
solely for mystics, and whether that category be taken
to include those still struggling in the Purgative Way
or only persons with experience of infused contemplation, it would not follow that none save those for
whom he was writing could profit by reading him.
An advanced treatise on music, physics or philosophy

---

[1] *Ascent*, Prologue (*Works*, I, 15). In his own times he was criti-
cized for this. Cf. *Studies*, I, 248, n. 3, and *Bulletin of Spanish
Studies*, Liverpool, 1942, XIX 179-81.

[2] *Dark Night*, Prologue (*Works*, I, 348).

[3] *Spiritual Canticle*, Prologue (*Works*, II, 25).

[4] *Living Flame*, Prologue (*Works*, III, 17).

will be not merely incomprehensible but completely devoid of interest to persons who, besides being without knowledge of music, physics or philosophy, neither intend nor desire to acquire any. But to those who know ever so little of the subject and (more important than that) are eager to learn more, it will not, however difficult, be wholly without meaning. Here and there, they can at least pick up hints, sense definitions, observe methods of argument and glimpse horizons which they may never reach but which it will give them joy to strive after. So, when Fitzmaurice-Kelly, in elaborating his perfectly accurate statement that St. John of the Cross is "of extreme obscurity to the profane," describes him as "incomprehensible to at least one layman whom I, for obvious personal reasons, would wish to regard as a person of average intelligence,"[5] he is judging, not St. John of the Cross, but himself. In fact, if he had turned over the very first page of the *Spiritual Canticle*, he would have found that his author had anticipated such a critic and told him just what he lacked:

These similitudes, if they be not read with the simplicity of the spirit of love and understanding embodied in them, appear to be nonsense.[6]

The truth is that the Saint is not comprehensible *solely*, but only *primarily*, to contemplatives. For any who will take the trouble to master his terminology,

[5] *Some Masters of Spanish Verse*, Oxford, 1924, p. 91.
[6] *Works*, II, 24.

his output in prose is not, as Fitzmaurice-Kelly asserts, "too subtle;" still less was it ever "intended (we are told) as a guide to highly trained confessors, expert casuists, deeply versed in the baffling arcana of moral theology."[7] "It is a relief," comments Fitzmaurice-Kelly, "to know this."[8] How we know it, and by whom "we are told" it, no indication is given. It is, of course, quite incorrect. St. John of the Cross himself makes it perfectly clear[9] that he was writing for simple friars and nuns, and not on "moral" but on "mystical" theology, "which is the science of love, and wherein these verities are . . . experienced."[10] He is anxious to help, not only "proficients"—and even that word does not mean confessors and casuists —but "beginners": *i.e.* those who are only practising *askesis* and have not got very far with that:

> To the end that all, *whether beginners or proficients,* may know how to commit themselves to God's guidance, when His Majesty desires to lead them onward, we shall give instruction and counsel, by His help, so that they may be able to understand His will, or, at the least, allow Him to lead them.[11]

It will be well here to touch first of all upon certain characteristics of beginners (which, although we treat

[7] *Some Masters,* etc., *loc. cit.*

[8] *Ibid.*

[9] The somewhat wild judgments quoted in the text, and the critic's reference (*loc. cit.*) to the Saint's four treatises as "*an* elaborate and voluminous commentary in prose" strongly suggest that he never read them.

[10] *Spiritual Canticle,* Prologue (*Works,* II, 25).

[11] *Ascent,* Prologue (*Works,* I, 12-13). Italics mine.

them with all possible brevity, will not fail to be of service likewise to the beginners themselves), in order that, realizing the weakness of the state wherein they are, they may take courage.[12]

So, even in the *Living Flame of Love*, he turns aside from his amazing theme to devote a digression many pages long to elementary topics. And elementary indeed they are. The early chapters of the *Ascent* and the *Dark Night* make it very clear how imperfect are the Saint's "beginners"—these "new lovers," as he terms them elsewhere, comparing them to "new wine . . . , for the fermentations of the wine of their love take place wholly without, in their senses."[13] Even the community at Beas, to judge from the nature of the "Cautions" which he addresses to them,[14] included not a few sisters whose places in the school of perfection were very low.

And the writings of St. John of the Cross have proved a help and an inspiration to countless others who would perhaps not even be called beginners— "ordinary" Christians, living hurried, active lives with little time for more than the barest obligations of their faith, yet evidently finding in these "incomprehensible" and "too subtle" treatises something applicable to their particular needs. What is this something? To what type of Christian, other than the contemplative, does St. John of the Cross appeal?

---

[12] *Dark Night,* I (*Works,* I, 350).
[13] *Spiritual Canticle,* XVI (Works, II, 99).
[14] *Works,* III, 220-6.

What message, if any, can this sublimest of mystics have for the world of to-day? These are questions which, at this time of world-wide agony, it is of peculiar interest to try to answer.

CHAPTER IV

Stumbling-blocks (I)

First, we may say with conviction that to the formal, half-hearted Christian he will make no appeal at all. With such a person he has nothing in common but a name. Nor does he attempt to cater for him. "We shall not here set down things that are . . . delectable," he announces, at the opening of the *Ascent of Mount Carmel*, "for all spiritual persons who desire to travel toward God by pleasant and delectable ways, but solid and substantial instruction."[1] Religiosity, spiritual self-indulgence, the "religion of the sacristy" enshrine vices, in his view, rather than virtues, and are displeasing to God. Those for whom he is writing, like those with whom he worked, are not "slothful or delicate souls, still less souls that are lovers of themselves."[2] His medicine is never emollient or sedative but tonic and astringent—and "delicate souls" reject such medicine, finding it bitter and painful. He sets before us two ways, the easy and the difficult; two ideals, pleasure and effort. We can choose which we like, but, if we choose the easy and pleasant, we are not for

[1] *Works*, I, 15.
[2] *Letters*, XVI (*Works*, III, 288).

him. "It is the most delicate flower," he warns us, "that soonest withers and loses its fragrance;" and, in another equally apt metaphor, he reminds us that "fruit that is both delicious and lasting is gathered in country that is cold and dry."[3]

> Wherefore beware thou of seeking to walk in the way of spiritual delight. . . . But choose thou for thyself spiritual vigour, and have attachment to naught, and thou shalt find sweetness and peace in abundance.[4]

What, then, of the genuine follower of Christ, who has no previous acquaintance with mystical writings or experience of the life of contemplation? It must be admitted that he, too, at first, has often scant sympathy with the Saint's teaching. The threefold Way, it seems to him, conforms hardly at all with his idea of Christianity: it must be meant for quite different people. To him being a Christian means the acceptance of certain dogmas; the practising of them, so far as they lend themselves to practice; attendance at Divine worship; the performance of certain other religious duties; the attempt to lead a moral life and possibly also to exercise a good influence upon those with whom one comes into contact. Anyone who does all that, in the general belief, does about as well as can be expected of him. And here is St. John of the Cross writing of God as of someone who can actually be known, and expecting us to prepare to make His acquaintance (and in this life, too!) by denying

[3] "Spiritual sentences and maxims," 39 (*Works*, III, 245).
[4] *Ibid.*

ourselves everything that makes life worth living—
not sins, mark you, or even pleasures of doubtful
legitimacy, but perfectly normal things, spiritual as
well as material, which good Christians everywhere
indulge in and are none the worse for. After renounc-
ing these, it appears, we begin to receive indications
of God's special nearness, and sometimes hear voices
speaking to us or see visions; but before long we
shall be plunged into terrible troubles of a spiritual
kind—this "Dark Night of the Spirit"—and the
very few who survive these will be rewarded by a
supreme experience described as "union," "transformation" or even "deification." It all sounds completely unlike the sober Christianity of the Church,
the Gospels and all the good people with whom we
are acquainted; it is all so far from the conventional
British standards of mediocrity and moderation.

The world presented to the average man by these
treatises, in short, is completely new, unfamiliar and
(to be frank) unattractive; nor does he become the
more reconciled to it on discovering that the "mystic" apparently spends a great part of his time in solitude, has little contact with his fellow-creatures, and
seems to lead a completely self-contained existence,
for which it is unlikely that anyone else will be very
much the better. Such a life seems to him almost
immoral. Can he really be understanding it all cor-
rectly?

When his eyes have at length grown accustomed

to the blackness of this new world and he begins to distinguish its outlines more clearly, the most outstanding feature causes him a positive repulsion. This is the Saint's teaching on detachment.

For that word, so he gathers from the *Ascent of Mount Carmel*, is interpreted to mean the complete annihilation of every kind of natural desire. The soul must be "deprived of the pleasure of its desire in all things"[5]—of every pleasure, that is to say, that comes to it through the five senses of sight, hearing, smell, taste and touch.[6] Beautiful sights, harmonious sounds or other kinds of attraction will present themselves—that is inevitable—but they must be rejected: and a man who deliberately keeps his eyes shut sees as little as a man born blind.[7] Whenever a choice presents itself, what is hard, unpleasant, mean, fatiguing and humbling must be preferred to what is easy, agreeable, precious, restful and exalting.[8] It is not enough to refrain from place-seeking; one must deliberately direct one's actions, words and even thoughts against one's own interests.[9] The ideal is to have no pleasures, no possessions and no knowledge, and the pursuit of this will apparently bring all pleasures, all possessions and all knowledge.[10]

The reference here is to detachment from sensual

[5] *Ascent*, I, iii (*Works*, I, 21).
[6] *Ibid*. (*Works*, I, 22).
[7] *Ibid*. (*Works*, I, 23).
[8] *Op. cit.*, I, xiii (*Works*, I, 61).
[9] *Ibid*. (*Works*, I, 62).
[10] *Ibid*. (*Works*, I, 62-3).

and exterior things, and this might well be thought
sufficiently drastic. But the more characteristic part
of the Saint's teaching also prescribes detachment
from spiritual things:

> The soul must not only be disencumbered from that
> which belongs to the creatures, but likewise, as it travels,
> must be annihilated and detached from all that belongs
> to its spirit.[11]

This counsel, he realizes, is revolutionary, and to
many "spiritual persons" will come as a shock:

> For they believe that any kind of retirement and re-
> formation of life suffices; and others are content with
> practising the virtues and continuing in prayer and
> pursuing mortification; but they attain not to detach-
> ment and poverty or denial or spiritual purity (which
> are all one). . . . They think that it suffices to deny them-
> selves worldly things without annihilating and purifying
> themselves of spiritual attachment. Wherefore it comes
> to pass that, when there presents itself to them any of
> this solid and perfect spirituality, consisting in the anni-
> hilation of all sweetness in God, in aridity, distaste and
> trial, which is the true spiritual cross, and the detach-
> ment of the spiritual poverty of Christ, they flee from it
> as from death, and seek only sweetness and delectable
> communion with God. This is not self-denial and de-
> tachment of spirit, but spiritual gluttony. Herein they
> become spiritually enemies of the cross of Christ.[12]

These are hard sayings, and, the more one thinks of
them, the harder they seem. They imply a self-strip-

[11] *Op. cit.*, II, vii (*Works*, I, 88).
[12] *Ibid.* (*Works*, I, 89). On spiritual gluttony, see *Dark Night*, I,
vi (*Works*, I, 364-5).

ping, not only of exterior aids to devotion, and of
dependence upon conditions favourable to prayer,
but even of "spiritual feelings," of the habit of culti-
vating a sense of God's presence and of the sensations
of spiritual well-being frequently described by the
mystics as "sweetness." They mean the rejection of
such "supernatural apprehensions" as visions and
locutions, even when one is convinced of their genuineness[13]—in other words, the rejection of God's
spiritual gifts, the possession of which is generally
considered, by Christian people not fortunate enough
to have them, as a sign of holiness. They mean, too,
at a certain stage of progress, an abandonment of
all intellectual activity: at this stage the soul must be
"voided and purified of all that is not God,"[14] and
therefore "free and disencumbered and at rest from
all knowledge and thought" and "without the ability
and without desire to have experience of (God) or to
perceive Him."[15]

That, stated briefly, is the first impression produced
by the teaching of St. John of the Cross on detachment: to be "detached from that which is without
and dispossessed of that which is within, and without attachment to the things of God."[16] Few persons,
however spiritually minded, will fail to find it repel-
lent. It strikes a deathly chill, not only into the unhealthy heat of sense-affection, but into the glowing

---

[13] *Ascent*, II, xvi, xix *(Works, I, 137, 155) et passim.*
[14] *Ascent*, II, vi *(Works, I, 86).*
[15] *Dark Night*, I, x *(Works, I, 379-80).*
[16] "Points of Love," 46 *(Works, III, 254).*

warmth of what one had hoped and believed to be pure love for God. It calls on one deliberately to go out from God-given light into a black and unknown darkness. Can such teaching, one asks, possibly be accepted by those who would be true Christians as a normal and a beneficial rule?

A third reason for the disenchantment experienced by many readers of the Saint's verses when they come to study other aspects of his life and writings is the part played in them by physical penance. Flagellations, hair-shirts and fasting to the point of endangering the health, they say, are completely *démodés*, relics from a barbarous past, which fail to achieve what they are supposed to do and in any case have been shown by science to be frequently inspired by motives and instincts the encouragement of which is anything but desirable.

Now as a matter of fact the idea that St. John of the Cross advocates widespread penances of this sort is quite an erroneous one, and, though very generally held, is probably derived from the accounts of his own life penned by pious hagiographers or from such writers as Vaughan, Inge and William James,[17] who, in their presentation of him as a grim and gloomy saint, have influenced others capable, if left to themselves and to his own writings, of interpreting him better. Too often, when the devout person thinks of the gentle little Carmelite saint, he visualizes the

[17] For characteristic quotations see R. L., pp. 40-1.

well-known caricature of him found in Huysmans'
novel, "terrible, sanglant et les yeux secs,"[18] or, as
Hoornaert puts it, "l'ascète horrible . . . celui qui
s'est arraché le coeur."[19]

Here he may be reassured. Whatever physical
austerities St. John of the Cross himself practised[20]—
and these, being a matter between himself and his
God, do not concern us—he makes very little mention of such things in his writings. His teaching can,
of course, be applied in that sense, as to any other
kind of asceticism; its main stress, however, is, not
on mortification of the flesh, but on mortification of
desire. In fact, on several occasions, he goes out of his
way to "lament the ignorance of certain men, who
burden themselves with extraordinary penances and
with many other voluntary practices, and think that
this practice or that will suffice to bring them to the
union of Divine Wisdom, *but such is not the case if
they endeavour not diligently to mortify their desires.*"[21] The best known and most striking passage
on the subject is actually a warning against excessive
physical penance, which the Saint describes as "ani-
mal penance" when it is performed to an immod-
erate extent, from motives of satisfaction to the
penitent and without the express approval of the
spiritual director. The passage is important enough
to be quoted in full:

[18] *En Route*, Paris, 1895, pp. 110-11.
[19] *L'Ame ardente de St. Jean de la Croix*, Bruges, 1928, pp. 19-20.
[20] Cf. p. 111.
[21] *Ascent*, I, viii (*Works*, I, 42-3). Italics mine.

Some of these persons, attracted by the pleasure which they find therein, kill themselves with penances, and others weaken themselves with fasts, by performing more than their frailty can bear, without the order or advice of any, but rather endeavouring to avoid those whom they should obey in these matters; some, indeed, dare to do these things even though the contrary has been commanded them.

These persons are most imperfect and devoid of reason; for they set bodily penance before subjection and obedience, which is penance of the reason and discretion, and therefore a sacrifice more acceptable and pleasing to God than any beside. But this, when the other side of it is disregarded, is no more than the penance of beasts, to which they are attracted, exactly like beasts, by the desire and pleasure which they find therein. Inasmuch as all extremes are sinful, and as in behaving thus such persons are working their own will, they grow in vice rather than in virtue; for, at the least, they are acquiring spiritual gluttony and pride in this way, through not walking in obedience. And many of these the devil assails, stirring up this gluttony in them through the pleasures and desires which he increases within them, to such an extent that, since they can no longer help themselves, they either change or vary or add to that which is commanded them, since any obedience in this respect is so bitter to them. To such depravity have some persons fallen that, simply because it is through obedience that they engage in these exercises, they lose the desire and devotion to perform them, their only desire and pleasure being to do what they themselves are inclined to do, so that it would probably be more profitable for them not to engage in these exercises at all.[22]

[22] *Dark Night*, I, vi (*Works*, I, 365-6).

Apart from allusions to the physical pain suffered in rapture[23] (which, being outside the subject's power of control, is beside the point) these are the only references to the subject in St. John of the Cross's writings: the objection may therefore be disposed of without further consideration.

Then there is a strange idea, which to a greater or a lesser extent seems to be held about all the mystics, that St. John of the Cross was a recluse who cared for nothing but the good of his own soul—to put it plainly, a thoroughly selfish person. This is probably attributable to his frequent use of such striking phrases as "Live in this world as though there were in it but God and thy soul, so that thy heart may be detained by naught that is human"[24]—a sentence which means, not that we should love God to the exclusion of our neighbour, but, as the final clause makes clear, that we must not allow our neighbour, or any other creature, to come between us and God. A striking example of this type of misinterpretation is to be found in Paul Elmer More, whose inability to understand Christian mysticism was quite remarkable. After making the astonishing statement that "the law of theistic mysticism is: In order to love God thou shalt not love thy neighbour," and rightly stigmatizing this position as "not only unscriptural

---

[23] E.g., *Spiritual Canticle*, XII (*Works*, II, 70).
[24] "Points of love," 61 (*Works*, III, 256). Cf. "Spiritual sentences and maxims," 25 (*Works*, III, 243).

but hateful,"[25] he snatches from their context and brings together a number of phrases from the *Ascent of Mount Carmel* which, he considers, "do not make pretty reading." They can be summed up in the maxim:

He that will love some other thing together with God of a certainty makes little account of God, for he weighs in the balance against God that which, as we have said, is far distant from God.[26]

He takes St. John's teaching to be that the two loves are "mutually exclusive," but this, of course, as the metaphor of the balance shows, is incorrect. "Love together with" means "love equally with," or "love in the same sense as." St. Paul's exhortation: "Set your affection on things above, not on things on the earth"[27] might similarly be interpreted: "You must love nothing but what is heavenly and have no love whatever for anything on earth." If the Colossians had so read the injunction, they too, presumably, would not have thought it "pretty reading." In precisely the same way the *Ascent of Mount Carmel* lays it down that "the soul that sets its affections upon creatures will be unable to comprehend God."[28] But it also teaches that anyone who would "attain to

[25] *Christian Mysticism*, London, 1932, pp. 73-4.

[26] *Ascent*, I, v (*Works*, I, 31). More uses (*op. cit.*, p. 74) an inferior translation, of which the "prettiness" is not increased by its use of the word "vile" for *bajo*, "low."

[27] Colossians ii². 2.

[28] *Ascent*, I, iv (*Works*, I, 25).

union with the infinite Being of God"[29] may love (in the sense of "having regard or affection for") creatures, provided such regard or affection does not come between them and what must be their main object: their love—that is, their supreme affection—for God.

Why, then, it may be asked, does St. John of the Cross say so little about such good works as helping one's neighbour? Because that was not his object. His theme being the road to union with God, his treatises can no more be expected to deal with human love than a treatise on human love can be expected to describe the road to union. But in private intercourse, we are told, he spoke of the Second Great Commandment very often:

> He would also say that love for the good of one's neighbour is born of the spiritual and contemplative life, and that, as this is commanded us by our Rule, it is clear we are also clearly commanded and charged to have this zeal for the profit of our neighbour.[30]

> He was accustomed to say that two things serve the soul as wings whereby it is able to rise to union with God: these are affective compassion for the death of Christ and for our neighbour.[31]

In his writings, too, there are a number of references of this kind; no careful student of St. John of the

[29] *Ibid.*

[30] "Spiritual sayings attributed to St. John of the Cross" (*Works*, III, 312).

[31] *Op. cit.*, p. 313.

Cross could possibly accuse him of indifference to his neighbour's welfare.

Good works, of whatever kind, play a clearly defined part in his system. Unlike the Illuminists and the Quietists, he considers them a normal part of the Christian life, but puts them on the level of meditations: neither will lead directly to Divine favours of a supernatural kind, though either is "a good preparation for them."

For it may come to pass that a person will have performed many good works, yet that He will not give him these touches of His favour; and another will have done far fewer good works, yet He will give him them to a most sublime degree and in great abundance.[32]

He warns us, too, following the Sermon on the Mount, not to do our good works in such a way as to be seen of men—and his penetrating remarks about this custom show that he knew a good deal about it.[33] We must hide them, not only from others, but even from ourselves—"that is to say . . . find no satisfaction in them, nor esteem them as if they were of some worth, nor derive pleasure from them at all."[34] "God alone" must see them.[35] What matters most is the love which lies beneath them: "they are the more excellent when they are performed with a purer and sincerer love of God, and when there is

[32] *Ascent*, II, xxxii (*Works*, I, 222).
[33] *Ascent*, III, xxviii (*Works*, I, 293-6).
[34] *Ibid.* (I, 295).
[35] *Ibid.*

less in them of self-interest, joy, pleasure, consolation
and praise, whether with reference to this world or
to the next."[36] In St, John of the Cross, indeed, the
whole question of good works is intimately bound
up with that of a love which "consists not of feeling
great things"[37] but expresses itself in actions—a love
directed towards God and overflowing on all sides
towards God's creatures. "It is clearly true," he used
to say, "that compassion for our neighbour grows the
more according as the soul is more closely united
with God through love; for the more we love, the
more we desire that this same God shall be loved
and honoured by all."[38] So "those of whom He takes
possession can never again be limited by their own
souls or contented with them. . . . Wherefore they
strive with yearnings and celestial affections and the
keenest diligence to bring many to Heaven with
them."[39] This saying gives a new meaning to that
beautiful but somewhat cryptic maxim: "At even-
tide they will examine thee in love."[40]

One final argument sometimes urged against St.
John of the Cross is that his language is often so
exaggerated as to be irreconcilable, not merely with
Christianity as commonly practised, but with the
teaching and example of Our Lord. This concerns

[36] *Ascent,* III, xxviii (*Works,* I, 293).
[37] "Points of love," 36 (*Works,* III, 253).
[38] "Spiritual sayings, etc." (*Works,* III, 312-13).
[39] *Op. cit.,* III, 313.
[40] "Spiritual sentences and maxims," 57 (*Works,* III, 247).

two of his themes in particular—Passivity and Transformation.

Into the subject of the Saint's teaching on Quiet, and his alleged condonation of quietism, I shall not attempt to enter here, though I hope one day to discuss it in detail. Molinos, contrarily to the usually held belief, made no use of St. John of the Cross in his *Spiritual Guide*, but his contemporaries, notably Falconi,[41] drew upon him freely and believed they were interpreting his doctrines. However, he has undoubtedly been fully acquitted of the charges of unorthodoxy which were made against his teachings after his death,[42] and in any case it is not really this that those who find his language on passivity a stumbling-block have in mind at all. Most of them have never heard of quietism: it merely seems to them that the Saint is advocating too negative a form of Christianity. For one thing, they dislike the continual emphasis which, as in the thirteenth chapter of the first book of the *Ascent*, and in many other parts of his writings, he lays upon the words "nothing," "nothingness" and "annihilation":

Endeavour that things be naught to thee, and that thou be naught to things.[43]

Blessed is that nothingness and blessed is that secret place of the heart that is of such great price that it possesses everything, yet desires to possess nothing. . . .[44]

[41] *Studies*, II, 347-92.
[42] Cf. *Works*, Appendix B (III, 382-434).
[43] "Points of love, 14" (*Works*, III, 251).
[44] *Letters*, XV (*Works*, III, 286-7).

[The soul] is withdrawn not only from all other things, but even from itself, and is annihilated.[45]

But even more than this they dislike the idea that the Christian should ever be anything but active. They like to think of their religion as something virile, positive and progressive, which achieves its results through God's blessing upon the Christian's ceaseless energy. And never has such an idea been more popular than in this present age of rush and excitement, of self-help and self-made men, in which each of us must take care of himself and the devil will take the hindmost. In the Passive Night of St. John of the Cross they are completely lost, though they are not sure how literally he wishes to be taken in such passages as these:

When the soul has completely purified and voided itself of all forms and images that can be apprehended, it will remain in this pure and simple light, being transformed therein into a state of perfection.[46]

If those souls . . . knew how to be quiet at this time, and troubled not about performing any kind of action, whether inward or outward, neither had any anxiety about doing anything, then they would delicately experience this inward refreshment in that ease and freedom from care.[47]

What they must do is merely to leave the soul free and disencumbered and at rest from all knowledge and thought, troubling not themselves, in that state, about

[45] *Spiritual Canticle*, XVII (*Works*, II, 105).
[46] *Ascent*, II, xv (*Works*, I, 129).
[47] *Dark Night*, I, ix (*Works*, I, 376).

what they shall think or meditate, but contenting themselves with no more than a peaceful and loving attentiveness toward God, and in being without anxiety, without the ability and without desire to have experience of Him or to perceive Him.[48]

It is clear that even the Saint's original readers sometimes found difficulty in his teaching here, for he has to deal at great length with people who fear that in practising Quiet they are "wasting their time"[49] and

think that all the business of prayer consists in experiencing sensible pleasure and devotion . . . ; strive to obtain this by great effort, wearying and fatiguing their faculties and their heads; and when they have not found this pleasure they become greatly discouraged, thinking that they have accomplished nothing.[50]

The first reply to this difficulty is that these and similar passages refer only to one stage in the mystical life and that it is as unreasonable to represent them as referring to its entire course as it would be to represent anyone who insists on the importance of relaxation as inculcating idleness. But one must also study the context of each passage, which will make it clear that what looks at first sight like passivity, in the sense of mental and spiritual idleness, is in reality activity in a very high degree. The soul has first to empty itself of all forms and images, but it does not then passively await the coming of any

48 *Op. cit.*, I, x (*Works*, I, 379-80).
49 *Dark Night*, I, x (*Works*, I, 380).
50 *Op. cit.*, I, vi (*Works*, I, 367).

and every impression: it holds itself in readiness, as it were—"in a peaceful and loving attentiveness"— for God to do His work in it. No activity, even on the human plane, is more of a strain than one of tautness, readiness, attentiveness. And in many passages St. John of the Cross makes it clear that there is activity of this kind:

> Here, as we say, the faculties . . . are working, not actively, but passively, by receiving that which God works in them; and, if they work at times, it is not with violence or with carefully · elaborated meditation, but with sweetness of love.[51]

> When the spiritual person cannot meditate, let him learn to be still in God, fixing his loving attention upon Him, in the calm of his understanding.[52]

Secondly, St. John of the Cross sometimes causes misgivings when he speaks of the transformation of the soul in God in the life of Union. Although he continually protests that anything he can say about this falls short of the truth:

> Were I to speak of it, it would seem less than it is. . . . [It] transcends all description and all sense. . . . For that reason I leave speaking of it here.[53]

the reader's protest is rather that the language he uses must be an exaggeration of the truth. As only those who have undergone a particular experience are fully qualified to pronounce upon a description

[51] *Ascent*, II, xii (*Works*, I, 113-4).
[52] *Ascent*, II, xv (*Works*, I, 129).
[53] *Living Flame*, IV (*Works*, III, 113).

of it, there would be a case for rejecting any such criticism outright. Furthermore, one of the arguments used by dissentients from this language is that it is unscriptural, and this is a point which can best be discussed later. But it may be well here to examine some typical passages and try to determine their true nature.

The first ground for this criticism is that the personality of the soul is represented as being lost when it is merged or "absorbed," in the Being of God—a misconception partly due, so far as English-reading people are concerned, to Arthur Symons' long-current mistranslation, in the "Dark Night," of Cesó todo y dejéme ("All ceased and I abandoned myself") as "All ceased, *and I was not.*" The second ground is that the soul is described as attaining "deification" which, one would think, ought to mean "becoming God":

that deification which it possesses, and the exaltation of the mind in God wherein it is as if enraptured, immersed in love, and become wholly absorbed in God, allows it not to take notice of any thing soever in the world.[54]

This is a most daring passage, but even here the use of the verb "possesses" and of the phrase "as if" implies the soul's retention of its personality. And my italics in the passages which follow, all of them typical of the Saint's teaching on the subject, will show how carefully guarded is his language, as one

[54] *Spiritual Canticle*, XVII (*Works*, II, 105). The second redaction (*Works*, II, 333) has: "immersed in love and wholly one with God."

would expect from a writer who, at the very beginning of the first of his treatises, went to such pains to make clear the incongruity between God and these creatures.[55]

> The soul . . . is at once illumined and transformed in God, and God communicates to it His supernatural Being, in such wise that it *appears to be* God Himself, and has all that God Himself has. . . . All the things of God and the soul are one *in participant transformation*; and the soul *seems to be* God rather than a soul, and is indeed God *by participation*; although it is true that its natural being, though thus transformed, *is as distinct from the Being of God as it was before.* . . .[56]

> [In] the consummation of this most happy estate of marriage with Him . . . is effected such union of the two natures and such communication of the Divine nature to the human that, while *neither of them changes its being*, each of them *appears to be God*.[57]

> The soul cannot reach this equality and completeness of love save by the total transformation of her *will* in that of God, wherein the two *wills* are united after such manner that they become one. And thus there is equality of love, for the will of the soul that is converted into the will of God is then wholly the will of God, and *the will of the soul is not lost* but becomes the will of God. And thus the soul loves God with the will of God, *which is also her own will.*[58]

> This thread of love binds the two—that is to say, God and the soul—with such firmness, and so unites and

[55] *Ascent*, I, iv.
[56] *Ascent*, II, v (*Works.* I, 82).
[57] *Spiritual Canticle*, XXVII (*Works.* II, 141).
[58] *Op. cit.*, XXXVII (*Works*, II, 172 3).

transforms them and makes them one in love, that, *although they differ in substance*, yet in glory and in appearance the soul *seems to be God* and God the soul.[59]

This soul . . . is transformed in God with such vehemence and is in so lofty a way *possessed of Him*.[60]

And when this Divine fire has transformed the substance of the soul into itself, *not only is the soul conscious of the burn*, but it has itself become one burn of vehement fire.[61]

The substance of the soul, although *it is not the Substance of God, for into this it cannot be changed*, is nevertheless united in Him and absorbed in Him, and is thus God *by participation* in God, which comes to pass in this perfect state of the spiritual life, although not so perfectly as in the next life.[62]

In other passages, which, taken, alone, might give a false impression, the context will make the exact sense clear. Thus, in the *Living Flame*, the Holy Spirit is described as penetrating "the soul continually, deifying its substance and making it Divine" and as absorbing "the soul, above all being, in the Being of God."[63] Yet the absorption is not complete, for the soul goes on to cry to God: "Break the web of this sweet encounter."[64] Contrast the figures of salt

[59] *Op. cit.*, XXXI (Second redaction) (*Works*, II, 358). For the simile of the fire and the dew, which occurs in the following paragraph, see p. 175, n. 65.
[60] *Living Flame*, I (*Works*, III, 19).
[61] *Ibid.* (*Works*, III, 41).
[62] *Living Flame*, II (*Works*, III, 57).
[63] *Living Flame*, I (*Works*, III, 38-9).
[64] *Ibid.*

dissolving in water and of rivers flowing into the ocean[65] which we find in the non-Christian, pantheistic mystics with the metaphors used by the Christian mystics for their descriptions of Union—the marriage, the two candle-flames, the window and the ray of sunlight, the log of wood in the fire. All these are continually used by St. John of the Cross, and none of them implies loss of personality, except that the log of wood is eventually united with the fire and becomes "one living flame within it."[66] But here St. John of the Cross guards himself by pointing out that even within Union there are degrees of perfection. The log on the fire is "transformed into fire and united with it," yet it long retains its individuality and "gives out sparks of fire and flame."[67]

While, therefore, it is possible to argue from St. John of the Cross that complete absorption within Union is possible, this can only be done by carrying a few of his statements to the farthest logical conclusion to which they will go. There is no doubt that the Saint believed in the retention of the individual personality and is most careful to make this evident.

[65] Cf. for example, *Himalayas of the Soul* (translations from the principal Upanishads by J. Mascaró), London, 1938, pp. 64, 78. The river-metaphor is once used by the Saint (*Works*, III, 35), but of love, not of the soul's personality. Perhaps the figure which brings St. John of the Cross nearest to pantheism is that of the fire and the dew (*Works*, II, 358) from the second redaction of the *Spiritual Canticle*. This, however, follows immediately upon a passage in which the orthodox position is most explicitly stated (cf. p. 174, n. 59).

[66] *Op. cit.*, Prologue (*Works*, III, 16-17).
[67] *Ibid.*

CHAPTER V

Stumbling-blocks (II)

HOW MUCH OF ST. JOHN'S TEACHING, after what has been said, may the Christian unfamiliar with the writings of the mystics still be expected to find difficult of acceptance? Only the first two of the stumbling-blocks described, I think, are still unsurmounted. The critic may continue to be puzzled by the apparent divergence of the mystic's standards from those of Christ and the Gospels, and by the demands with which he appears to be faced for a seemingly impossible degree of detachment. If those two difficulties can be overcome, the remainder should automatically disappear, while at the same time certain aspects of the Saint's thought should begin to exercise upon him an unsuspected and an irresistible appeal. Let us see, then, how upon closer examination these obstacles vanish.

First, although it is true that the doctrine of St. John of the Cross conflicts with many of the practices and tendencies of current Christianity, it is the latter, and not the former, if measured by the standards of Holy Scripture, that will be found wanting. In the "widespread, minimized and vulgarized conception of Christianity which is common to our day," remarks a modern commentator, there is hardly a single fundamental point of whole-hearted agreement "with the basic truths contained in the New Testament and accepted by St. John as the foundation of all his teaching."[1] Reference has already been made to the constant dependence of the Saint upon the Scriptures. But such a phrase as that gives little or no idea of the extent to which these four treatises, the poems on which they are based, and such minor works as the *Letters* and *Maxims* are soaked and steeped in a knowledge, understanding and love of the Bible and impregnated and permeated with the spirit of the Divine Master. It was not by chance that of the only two books which the Saint allowed himself to keep in his cell one was a Bible.[2] Any who believe that Catholics know nothing of their Bible might find it a salutary exercise to take a single page —almost any page—of St. John of the Cross and disengage from it, not merely quotations, but all the references, allusions and passages which depend upon Biblical sources.

This being so, it is unlikely, on the face of it, that the doctrine of the Saint will be out of harmony with that of the Bible, especially as, at the beginning of his first treatise, it is on the Bible that he pledges himself to base his doctrine; "for, if we guide ourselves by this, we shall be unable to stray, since He Who speaks therein is the Holy Spirit."[3] Similarly in

[1] Frost, pp. 26-7.
[2] *Works*, III, 376.
[3] *Ascent*, Prologue (*Works*, I, 11).

the *Spiritual Canticle* ("I think not to affirm aught that is mine . . . unless it be confirmed and expounded by authorities from the Divine Scripture")[4] and, more briefly, in the *Living Flame*. Actually, examination soon shows that all these works harmonize with Scripture in every particular.

Let us take as an example the teaching of St. John on the Being of God. The Biblical conception of God ought to be familiar to every Christian, though actually it has been so much attenuated by popular theology that a full synthetic presentation of it would shatter many a churchgoer's complacency. God, in Holy Scripture, is "the everlasting God, the Lord, the Creator of the ends of the earth"; "Light, and in Him is no darkness at all"; All-Holy, before Whom no man can stand; All-Powerful, than Whom no other reigns; All-Wise, His judgments unsearchable and His ways past finding out; All-Loving, untrammelled in His love by man's unworthiness; "the blessed and only Potentate, the King of kings, and Lord of lords, Who only hath immortality . . . Whom no man hath seen, nor can see." He dwells, "not in temples made with hands," but "in the light which no man can approach unto." A Spirit, He must be worshipped "in spirit and in truth."[5]

Is this the God Whom many Christians so seldom approach, pausing, when they do so, hardly for a

[4] *Spiritual Canticle*, Prologue (*Works*, II, 25).
[5] Isaiah xl. 28; 1 St. John i. 5; 1 Samuel vi. 20; Revelation xix. 6; Romans xi. 33; 1 Timothy vi. 15.

moment to recollect themselves in His presence before rushing on to ask Him to satisfy their predominantly temporal necessities? We may have a certain degree of love for Him, but at best most of us love created things as much or more: few give Him the first place. How often we have the presumption to address Him in a few glib words hardly coming from the mind at all or even to worship Him with a mere posture of the body, the heart and the thoughts being elsewhere! How often we attempt to make conditions with Him, offer Him a strictly reserved allegiance, call in question His unsearchable judgments, ask why He has not abolished war, poverty, evil, pain! This God so casually approached is no God at all, but as much an idol of our own invention as any worshipped in a heathen temple. "The workman made it; therefore it is not God."[6]

But St. John of the Cross, singing, as indeed he may:

> How well I know the fount that freely flows ... !
> The eternal fount its source has never show'd,
> But well I know wherein is its abode.[7]

leads us back to the true and Biblical conception of the Godhead. His God is the true God: the First and the Last,[8] "Infinite Being" beside Whom "all the being of creation is nothing;"[9] incomprehensible and

[6] Hosea viii. 6.
[7] *Works*, II. 454.
[8] *Ascent*, II, ii, xxvi (*Works*, I, 68, 196).
[9] *Ascent*, I, iv (Works, I, 25).

inaccessible to man's natural imagination and under-standing;[10] "coming within no image or form"[11] and thus essentially "strange," not only "to men who have never seen Him," but even to the holy angels;[12] "omnipotent, wise, good, merciful, just, strong and loving," with "other infinite attributes and virtues whereof we have no knowledge here below."[13]

From this conception of God follows the Saint's characteristic conception of the soul's quest for God. Since creation, beside God, is "nothing," "the soul that sets its affections upon the being of creation is likewise nothing in the eyes of God, and less than nothing. . . . And therefore such a soul will in no wise be able to attain to union with the infinite Being of God; for that which is not can have no agreement with that which is."[14] How ridiculous, then, to try "to measure God by the measure of your own capacity,"[15] or to bracket God in the affections with creatures, when "He is at an infinite distance from them all"![16]

Inasmuch as there is naught that equals God, the soul that loves some other thing together with Him, or clings to it, wrongs Him greatly. And if this is so, what would it be doing if it loved anything more than God?[17]

[10] *Letters*, XI (*Works*, III, 279-81); *Ascent*, II, xii (*Works*, I, 111).
[11] *Ascent*, II, xvi (*Works*, I, 133).
[12] *Spiritual Canticle*, XIII (*Works*, II, 78).
[13] *Living Flame*, III (*Works*, III, 60).
[14] *Ascent*, I, iv (*Works*, I, 25).
[15] *Letters*, III (*Works*, III, 266).
[16] *Ascent*, III, xii (*Works*, I, 249).
[17] *Ascent*, I, v (*Works*, I, 31).

Meditation upon the creatures, which reflect and declare God's glory, may take the soul, a little way towards a knowledge of the Creator: it is, in fact, "after the practice of self-knowledge . . . the first thing in order upon this spiritual road to the knowledge of God."[18] But, beyond a determinable point upon that road, the creatures begin to obscure God's image, and then the instruction to the soul must be:

Take thou no heed of the creatures if thou wilt keep the image of God clearly and simply in thy soul, but empty thy spirit of them, and withdraw far from them, and thou shalt walk in the Divine light; for God is not like to the creatures.[19]

Once we have regained the true Biblical conception of God, all this follows naturally from it. Such a downright maxim as "All for Thee and naught for me"[20] may seem over-exacting, but how can one escape from it save by rejecting the precept of the Old Law, specifically endorsed by Christ: "Thou shalt love the Lord thy God with *all* thy heart, and with *all* thy soul, and with *all* thy strength." And this, we must remember, is "the first of all the commandments."[21]

What has been said of St. John's teaching on the Being of God could of course be developed at much greater length, and it is unlikely that any of it would be found to deviate in the slightest degree from

[18] *Spiritual Canticle*, IV (*Works*, II, 46).
[19] "Spiritual Sentences and Maxims," 25 (*Works*, III, 243).
[20] "Points of love," 32 (*Works*, III, 252).
[21] St. Mark xii. 30. Cf. Deuteronomy vi. 5.

Scripture. The same is true of the rest of his doctrine: whatever parts of it be examined, including those least acceptable to the average reader, they will be found to rest upon the same sure foundation. The difference between the popular attitude to the "hard sayings" of Our Lord and to those of St. John of the Cross is that the former, having been uttered nearly two thousand years ago to an Eastern people, are taken as being figurative and either diluted, or discounted, or simply disregarded altogether, whereas the latter, being less than four hundred years old and belonging to our own Western civilization, cannot be so easily passed over.

But if, for example, we take the "lines which are written in the Ascent of the Mount,"[22] since these have so often provoked criticism, we find that they are hardly more than a re-statement and an expansion of the First Beatitude. What is the maxim:

> In order to arrive at possessing everything,
> Desire to possess nothing.[23]

unless perhaps a variant of the Pauline "Having nothing, and yet possessing all things,"[24] but a paraphrase of:

> Blessed are the poor in spirit [they who possess nothing]: for theirs is the kingdom of heaven [for they shall possess everything]?[25]

[22] *Ascent*, I, xiii (*Works*, I, 62).
[23] *Ibid.* (*Works*, I, 63).
[24] 2 Corinthians vi, 10.
[25] St. Matthew v. 3. An even closer parallel will be found in *Letters*, XV (*Works*, III, 286).

The reminder that

> In order to pass from the all to the All,
> Thou hast to deny thyself wholly in all[26]

is a re-enunciation of the Divine paradox: "Whosoever will save his life shall lose it: and whosoever will lose his life for my sake shall find it."[27] The couplet

> For if thou wilt have anything in all [*sc.* creatures]
> Thou hast not thy treasure purely in God.[28]

merely re-states the antithesis made by Christ between "treasures upon earth" and "treasures in Heaven," and tells us, as He told us, that where our treasure is, there will our heart be also.[29] There is nothing more Scriptural than the teaching of this much discussed chapter.

And in all the pronouncements of St. John of the Cross on detachment we find the same dependence upon Biblical truths which, being unpalatable to many professing Christians, are liable to be explained away. There is the Biblical conception of the strait gate, the narrow way, the few that find it, the many called, the few chosen.[30] The teaching that the way to God is the way of the Cross,[31] of which

---

[26] *Ascent*, I, xiii (*Works*, I, 63).

[27] St. Matthew xvi. 25. This text is actually discussed when the subject is taken up again in *Ascent*, II, vii (*Works*, I, 89-90).

[28] *Ascent*, I, xiii (*Works*, I, 63).

[29] St. Matthew vi. 19-21. Cf. *Ascent*, III, ii (*Works*, I, 227-8).

[30] St. Matthew vii. 14; xx. 16.

[31] St. Matthew xvi. 24.

the Saint remarks: "It may almost be said that, the more necessary it is for spiritual persons, the less it is practised by them."[32] The Pauline injunction to cleanse ourselves from all filthiness of the flesh *and spirit*.[33] The assurance: "If ye then be risen with Christ . . . ye are dead and your life is hid with Christ in God."[34] The aim of the Christian: nothing less than perfection—an aim inculcated by Christ:

Be ye therefore perfect, even as your Father which is in Heaven is perfect.[35]

and in the Epistles, especially in those of St. Paul.[36]

In the advice upon detachment which the Saint gave to his spiritual daughters, the voice of Christ is heard so clearly that to quote Biblical parallels would be superfluous. "Unnatural" or "unpractical" the dilettante in religion may call it, but no one can deny that it is Scriptural:

For all persons thou shalt have equal love and equal forgetfulness, whether they be thy relatives or no. . . . Hold them all as strangers to thee.[37]

Have no care for [possessions]—neither as to food, nor clothing, nor any other created thing, nor as to the morrow. Thou must direct this care to something higher, namely, to seeking the kingdom of God.[38]

[32] *Ascent*, II, vii (*Works*, I, 88).
[33] 2 Corinthians vii. 1.
[34] Colossians iii. 1, 3.
[35] St. Matthew v. 48. Cf. xix. 21; St. John xvii. 23.
[36] E.g., 2 Corinthians xii. 9; xiii. 11; Philippians iii. 15; Colossians i. 28; iv. 12; 2 Timothy iii. 17.
[37] "Cautions," 6 (*Works*, III, 221).
[38] "Cautions," 7 (*Works*, III, 221) .

Never fail to perform any good works because of the lack of pleasure or sweetness that thou findest therein, if it be fit that they should be done in the service of Our Lord.[39]

Another subject on which the Saint's teaching must have been unacceptable to a great many devout Spaniards, as it will also be to many of his readers to-day, is the use of aids to devotion.[40] Little is said about these in the Scriptures, and St. John advocates them with no great enthusiasm,[41] for "the person who is truly devout sets his devotion principally upon that which is invisible,"[42] though they are "certainly lawful, and even expedient, for beginners,"[43] provided always they be not abused. Connected with this subject is the use of special places for prayer, and here St. John recalls that Our Lord not only worshipped in the Temple, but, for His private prayers, used to "choose solitary places . . . and such as occupied the senses but little . . . , places that lifted up the soul to God, such as mountains."[44] Accordingly he recommends his readers to do so too. At the same time he quotes the principle laid down by Christ in His instruction to the woman of Samaria.[45] The "truly spiritual man"

[39] "Cautions," 16 (*Works*, III, 225).

[40] Some reflections on this and related subjects will be found in *Bulletin of Spanish Studies*, Liverpool, 1942, XIX, 178-86.

[41] *Ascent*, III, xxxvff. (*Works*, I, 309ff).

[42] *Ibid.* (I, 311).

[43] *Ibid.* (I, 321). Cf. *Ascent*, III, xxiv (*Works*, I, 283): "and indeed should."

[44] *Ascent*, III, xxxix (*Works*, I, 322). Cf. p. 195.

[45] St. John iv. 23-4. Cf. *Ascent*, II, xxxix (*Works*, I, 321)

is never bound to a place of prayer which is in any way convenient, nor does he even consider this, for that would be to remain bound to sense.[46]

As to the matter and form of prayer, the model of prayers, for Him, as for all Christians, is the Pater Noster. His argument is simple:

> It is clear that, when His disciples besought Him that He would teach them to pray, He would tell them all that is necessary in order that the Eternal Father may hear us, as He knew His nature so well. Yet all that He taught them was the Pater Noster, with its seven petitions, wherein are included all our needs, both spiritual and temporal; and He taught them not many other kinds of prayer, either in words or in ceremonies.[47]

We, therefore, must not "let the will be set upon other ceremonies and forms of prayer than those which Christ taught us."[48]

Coming now to mystical experience, and setting aside such supernormal phenomena as visions, locutions and raptures, for which there is abundant Scriptural evidence and to which St. John of the Cross often refers, we may consider briefly some Biblical parallels for his accounts of the Life of Union and of the transformation of the soul in God. In general, he draws mainly on his own experiences, and but lightly on Scripture, refraining from using a number of passages, both in the Gospels and in the

[46] *Ibid.* (*Works*, I, 322).

[47] *Ascent*, III, xliv (*Works*, I, 330).

[48] *Ibid.* The whole paragraph follows the teaching of the Sermon on the Mount very closely.

Epistles, to which minor writers on mystical theology make frequent, and perhaps excessive, appeal. Several times, however, he echoes the language, not only of St. Paul but of Christ Himself, as recorded in the Fourth Gospel. In one part of the *Spiritual Canticle*, while not specifically asserting that St. Paul's "I live, yet not I, but Christ liveth in me" refers to the Spiritual Marriage, he claims that St. Paul's "life was not his own, because he was transformed in Christ and his life was Divine rather than human." He also uses mystical terminology in speaking of a "union of love," in which "the Beloved lives in the lover and the lover in the Beloved," so that "it may be said that each is the other and that both are one."[49] In another place he directly relates this passage with the Spiritual Marriage, where "the soul enjoys and perceives the delight and glory of God in its very substance, which is now transformed in Him."[50]

Elsewhere[51] he glosses words of Our Lord:

That they all may be one; as Thou, Father, art in Me, and I in Thee, that they also may be one in Us. . . . That they may be one, even as We are one: I in them, and Thou in Me, that they may be made perfect in one.[52]

[49] *Spiritual Canticle*, XI (*Works*, II, 68).
[50] *Op. cit.*, XXVII (*Works*, II, 141-2).
[51] *Spiritual Canticle*, XXXVIII (*Works*, II, 177).
[52] St. John xvii. 21-3. I do not know on what grounds P. E. More (*Christian Mysticism*, London, 1932, p. 49) bases his assertion that neither this passage nor Galatians ii. 20 refers to mystical Union.

interpreting them as referring to "union by participation," but also remarking that the meaning of the passage is not that the saints "are to be one thing in essence and nature, as are the Father and the Son, but rather that they may be so by union of love, as are the Father and the Son in unity of love. Wherefore souls possess these same blessings by participation as He possesses by nature; for the which cause they are truly gods by participation, equals of God and His companions."[53] St. Paul's language to the Galatians and the Colossians suggests that the early Christians interpreted these passages similarly. It seems to me, in short, that, both in this particular restrained use of Holy Scripture, and elsewhere in his works, St. John of the Cross directly challenges those who do not accept his interpretations to the words of Christ and the Apostles. If they reject these, how do they themselves interpret Our Lord? And if they paraphrase or dilute His words, are they sure that they are not doing so in order to escape the consequences of a literal interpretation? St. John's highly spiritual exegeses of Scripture should surely not be unacceptable to those who find reality in things of the spirit, and he must indeed be a self-assured Christian who can lightly dismiss them as erroneous.

Our Lord's words are surely susceptible of that interpretation, among others, while St. Paul undoubtedly enjoyed supernormal experiences (Acts ix; 2 Corinthians xii) and seems to me quite frequently to be referring to such experiences.

[53] *Works*, II, 177.

The objector might seem to be on firmer ground when he queries the Saint's teaching on detachment —even on detachment from sense. Is it practical, he asks, for everyone to crucify the pleasures of sense, to renounce the love for kindred, to make a consistent choice of the difficult rather than the easy, to develop a positive ambition to be despised and unknown? Can any society cohere on such a basis? And supposing that it can, is it really the will of God that it should?

These questions, I think, indicate a misunderstanding of the Saint's teaching, in at least one important particular. It has already been shown that he was writing, not solely, but largely, for advanced contemplatives, and it is to these that he addresses his austerest counsels. The society, in other words, in which sense is to be crucified and ambition to be directed towards self-abasement is a society of persons who, of their free will, have withdrawn from the world and set themselves as their chief aim the attainment of union on earth with God. If withdrawal from the world meant no more than bodily retirement within four walls, such ideals might be as unintelligible to religious as to anyone else: the nuns of the Incarnation, for example, would probably have made little more of the lines on the "Ascent of the Mount" than the courtiers of Philip II. But from any community, or from any individual, striving towards union with God the inflexible logic of the Saint's two great ascetic treatises will command immediate assent.

To such the deductions drawn from his doctrine on the Being of God will seem perfectly natural. Many, indeed, will themselves have made them in their very act of self-dedication to the life of prayer. God has revealed Himself to them as the All, the only Reality; and forthwith the creatures have sunk back into their proper position of an insignificance so supreme that it can most accurately be described as one of "nothingness." The sole thing, then, that matters to them will be the quest for God: the Saint's strictures upon creature-ambitions can only be in the nature of reminders, for they will already have made them their own.

Detachment from spiritual things is a more advanced conception than detachment from sense, but it follows just as logically from the premises already enunciated. It is surely reasonable that there should come a point when a soul striving after pure Spirit should be called upon to make a complete surrender to pure Spirit. Throughout the progress of such a soul, sweetness in prayer will be as much a hindrance as sweet food; there is no essential difference between a physical attachment to a brother or sister in the world and a spiritual attachment to a brother or sister in the cloister; and there comes a time, even to others than religious, when images, incense and music are greater obstacles to spiritual progress than novels and theatre-tickets, because these latter have ceased to have the slightest attraction.

No one who is engaged upon the supreme quest will think St. John of the Cross too severe a teacher. What he has done is to remove boulders from the path or to show how they may be avoided. When the contemplative looks at the "Mount of Perfection," his eyes will immediately fasten upon the summit, "whereon dwells the glory and honour of God." In the couplets, it is upon the "Everything," the "All," that his mind seizes, not upon the "anything," the "all," which he must renounce in order to attain to it. What makes it reasonable, in other words, to demand such great sacrifice is that it will bring an incomparably greater gain.

Not only, then, is all this asceticism and renunciation intended solely for the traveller on the Mystic Way, but even for him it is always a means to an end. The athlete's training, when he details it to a layman, sounds gloomy and uninspiring enough: it is only the thought of the contest for which he is preparing that illumines it and gives it meaning. He lives in conditions which, were there no good reason for doing so, he would find intolerable; but to win his race he would be glad, like old Antonio faced with the prospect of Duruelo, to live in a pigsty. The Christian, until he reads the mystics (or unless he cannot believe them), may harbour doubts as to the possibility of attaining Union, but he will hardly maintain that the game is not worth the candle—or, to use a more appropriate figure, that the dawn is not worth the Dark Night.

If these considerations, as is to be hoped, have justified to the reader St. John's insistence upon the need for complete detachment of sense and spirit, his question will now be: What does he say to me? The answer must depend upon the questioner's aim. To the extent that he shares the mystic's ideal, he must share the mystic's sacrifice. If he is a genuine "beginner"—if, that is, he hopes to climb at least the lower slopes of the Mount of Perfection; if he is led from his house by God, "enkindled in love of Him, upon a dark night," that very act of setting forth implies a "privation and purgation of all (his) sensual desires, with respect to all outward things of the world and to those which were delectable to its flesh, and likewise with respect to the desires of its will."[54] Even as definite a phrase as this can be variously interpreted, and the Saint would no doubt say that the exact interpretation must be left to the director, or to whatever other spiritual guide one may choose. Some may take no guide but the Scriptures and the teaching of the Church: on them will fall the responsibility of interpreting the *Ascent of Mount Carmel* for themselves. The one conclusion, however, which none can escape is that renunciation is inseparable from progress. Is that too hard a lesson for our day and age? It surely ought not to be.

[54] *Ascent,* I, i (*Works,* I, 18).

We can form a more detailed opinion than this, however, upon the degree of sacrifice which the Saint would demand of every genuine, practising Christian. "All the desires," he says, "are not equally hurtful, nor do they all equally embarrass the soul": to mortify the natural desires completely in this life is impossible.[55] His standpoint—one often adopted by the mystics, especially by those who say less of the higher stages of the Mystic Way—is that up to a certain point, if wisely used, the creatures serve as a revelation of God. On one of those last pages of the unfinished third Book of the *Ascent* in which, for the especial benefit of the "beginner," he permits himself a digression, he "proposes a test" by which we may know when pleasures of sense are profitable and when they are not.

... It is that, whensoever a person hears music and other things, and sees pleasant things, and is conscious of sweet perfumes, or tastes things that are delicious, or feels soft touches, if his thought and the affection of his will are at once centred upon God and if that thought of God gives him more pleasure than the movement of sense which causes it, and save for that he finds no pleasure in the said movement, this is a sign that he is receiving benefit therefrom, and that this thing of sense is a help to his spirit. In this way such things may be used, for then such things of sense subserve the end for which God created and gave them, which is that He should be the better loved and known because of them.[56]

[55] *Ascent*, I, xi (*Works*, I, 51).
[56] *Ascent*, III, xxiv (*Works*, I, 284).

Quite a sufficiently stringent test, it might be thought, for persons living in the world, but hardly too exacting for those who try to "keep the image of God clearly and simply" in their soul. It would be difficult for any realist to find fault with the generalizations that, when the condition laid down is not observed, delight in visible things may lead (for example) to vanity, distraction and envy; delight "in hearing useless things," to "gossiping, envy, rash judgments and vacillating thoughts"; delight in "sweet perfumes," to "loathing of the poor"; delight in food, to gluttony, ill-health and spiritual torpor; and delight "in the touch of soft things," to "many more evils and more pernicious ones, which . . . quench all spiritual strength and vigour."[57] The test laid down, though not perhaps always easy to apply, would eliminate a good many of these dangers, and, more important still, preserve and intensify the subject's spiritual sensibility.

With regard to a number of pleasures, it is possible to enter into greater detail. Nature, for example, as we have seen, was highly attractive to St. John of the Cross himself, and we have both direct and indirect indications that he thought of it as a positive help to devotion: unlike St. Bernard, who is said to have walked along the banks of Lake Leman without raising his eyes to the beauties around him, he would willingly allow it a place in his consciousness. Indeed, his view, expressed in his own quaint lan-

[57] *Ascent*, III, xxv (*Works*, I, 285-7).

guage, is that God makes use of "a pleasing effect of variety, whether obtained by the arrangement of the ground or of trees," to "move the will to devotion." Applying the test just proposed, he concludes that such spots should be used for devotion "if they at once lead the will to God and cause it to forget the places themselves."[58] To such Divine forgetfulness we owe the profundity of the "Spiritual Canticle." In the gloom of the prison at Toledo the Saint had pondered earnestly on his memories of flower-strewn meadows, lonely wooded valleys, rushing rivers, gentle breezes, tranquil nights and the soft approach of the dawn.. With the beauties of the Andalusian countryside unveiled before him, he was, perhaps surprisingly, less original in his evocations of Nature, but in and out of those serene and sunny stanzas run the three themes of woods, hills and water in a way that leaves no doubt how frequently they recurred to his imagination. Never is St. John of the Cross happier and more human, yet never more sublime, than when he writes of Nature.

As to music, the classical passage is to be found in the *Spiritual Canticle*, and its being metaphorical does not dispel the impression which we have gained from the Saint's biography that he was a genuine music-lover: anyone else, indeed, would hardly have introduced the double theme of "silent music" and "sounding solitude" into a poem of pure imagination. The *Ascent of Mount Carmel* first refers to the

[58] *Ascent*, III, xlii (*Works*, I, 324-5).

ear which is delighted by "a concert of music or a peal of bells" and goes on to apply to delight in music a test very similar to that already laid down for other forms of sense-pleasure:

Little does it matter that one kind of music should sound better than another if the better kind move me not more than the other to do good works.[59]

It is perhaps surprising that St. John of the Cross should go as fully as he does[60] into the use of such aids to devotion as images, rosaries, oratories and ceremonies, all of which he seems to class as much with Nature and music as with novenas and sermons. Presumably the religious for whom he wrote were given to indulgence, or even to over-indulgence, in these accessories and practices, and he was anxious to wean them from a more formal to a more spiritual use of them.

It will suffice if we summarize the Saint's views on the use of images—the accessory discussed at greatest length—as these are identical in principle with his opinions on the rest. He begins by warmly defending their use against "those pestilent men" (presumably the Illuminists), who, "inspired by Satanic pride and envy," have tried to abolish them.[61] "There can be no deception or peril" in their proper use, "because naught is esteemed therein other than that which is represented."[62] The important thing (and this is

[59] *Ascent*, III, xlv (*Works*, I, 333).
[60] Cf. pp. 185-6.
[61] *Ascent*, III, xv (*Works*, I, 257).
[62] *Ibid.* (*Works*, I, 258). Cf. also I, 310.

repeated several times in varying phraseology) is to apply the principle with which by this time we shall be familiar—to forget the image and think only of what it represents:

We exhort men to pass beyond that which is painted that they may not be hindered from attaining to the living truth beneath it, and to make no more account of the former than suffices for attainment to the spiritual.[63]

Images, like Nature and music, are means to an end: when they are made an end in themselves, they become dangerous. Though images should never be "so ill-carved that they take away devotion rather than inspire it,"[64] we should consider their truth and lifelikeness rather than "the value and cunning of their workmanship and decoration;"[65] for, if we think only of this last, "sense is pleased and delighted, and the love and rejoicing of the will remain there. This is a complete hindrance to true spirituality."[66]

Enlarging upon this theme,[67] the Saint criticizes those who dress up images in fashionable clothes as though they were dolls; who have "more confidence in one kind of image than in another;" who become attached to particular images; and so on. But his real concern is that this and other aids to devotion shall

---

[63] *Ibid.*
[64] *Ascent*, III, xxxviii (*Works*, I, 318).
[65] *Ascent*, III, xxxv (*Works*, I, 310).
[66] *Ibid.*
[67] *Ascent*, III, xxxv-xxxvii (*Works*, I, 310-17), *passim*

be used only by those not far enough advanced to do without them: [68]

> The person who is truly devout . . . needs few images and uses few. . . . Nor is his heart attached to the images that he uses; if they are taken from him, he grieves very little, for he seeks within himself the living image, which is Christ crucified.[69]

Enough will have been said to show that, while requiring the highest conceivable standard of detachment from those advancing toward the highest conceivable goal, St. John of the Cross makes fewer demands of less advanced contemplatives, of those setting out on the road, and, we may be sure, of persons living in the world. He tries to inspire all his readers with spiritual ambition, shows them the desirability of a higher goal than they are aiming at and urges them to "raise up their desires above childish things"[70] so that they may catch a glimpse of it, if only from afar. But the idea that he makes impossible demands on everybody is a sheer legend. Austere and forbidding though his treatises may seem when we merely turn over their pages, as soon as we begin to study them in detail we find them full of serenity, beauty and understanding.

[68] Cf. p. 185, n. 43.
[69] *Ascent*, III, xxxv (*Works*, I, 311).
[70] *Ascent*, I, v (*Works*, I, 31).

Attractiveness of His Teaching

S̲O WE HAVE ANSWERED the objections which the "ordinary Christian" may make to St. John of the Cross's teaching. Let us now look at the other side of the picture and consider the positive attractions which it may hold for him, particularly at the present time.

First, this Saint restores, to a world which had nearly lost it, a sense of the transcendence of Almighty God. This is not to say that he loses sight for a moment of the Divine immanence, a subject which no mystical work treats with more delicacy and insight than the *Spiritual Canticle*. But the overpowering impression produced by the terms in which he speaks of God is one of awe. Upon his realization of God's greatness, as we have shown, depends his whole system; and, although by Divine grace he was himself enabled to attain mystical Union, and urges others to strive for the same goal, he never allows his conception of God to be attenuated by the intimacy of his communion with Him.

It is, on the contrary, in his *Living Flame of Love*, the work in which he has the most to say of this most intimate communion, that he conveys the most vivid impression of God's infinite greatness. Nowhere does he create a deeper hush of receptive reverence than in his commentary on the stanza beginning "Oh, lamps of fire . . ." in which the attributes of God— omnipotence, wisdom, holiness, and all the rest— shed the soft radiance of many and wondrous lamps over the soul's faculties, and yet, at the same time, combine in the "one and simple Being" of the God-head.[1] Each of these attributes, in fact, is "the very Being of God in one single simple reality," and in each of them "He gives light and burns as God."[2] Thus, although there is a way in which the soul can approach God, this way is not the use of its unaided faculties. For

God, towards whom the understanding is journeying, transcends the understanding and is therefore incomprehensible and inaccessible to it; and thus, when it is understanding, it is not approaching God, but is rather withdrawing itself from Him.[3]

As we read such passages as these, we realize, perhaps with a shock, how far our conception of God has strayed from that which we find in Holy Scripture. Popular theology, for generations past, has been insisting more and more upon the "divinity of man," and upon "God's need of man," with the result that we have grown more and more oblivious of our own insufficiency and of God's majesty. We have attempted to make God complementary to ourselves, to take

---

[1] *Living Flame*, III (*Works*, III, 59ff.).
[2] *Ibid.* (*Works*, III, 60).
[3] *Ibid.* (Second redaction) (*Works*, III, 186).

Him into collaboration with us, to think of Him as aiding us, at our request, in what we do—at any rate if it meets with His approval. So accessible have we believed His spiritual gifts to be that we have asked for them in mere forms of words, sometimes even unquickened by any reality of desire, and wondered why they have not reached us. It is remarkable if we have not presumed to think of mystical Union itself as something to be had for the asking: we are certainly apt to take it for granted that, when this life is over, we, with all our friends, and just because they are our friends, shall go to Heaven.

St. John of the Cross, like St. Augustine, impresses upon us continually a vivid realization of man's littleness and God's greatness—"l'infiniment grand et l'infiniment petit"—and by so doing corrects our unworthy and presumptuous actions, strikes us dumb with the sense of our own nothingness and drives us to our knees in adoration and awe. The experience, humiliating though it be, is also purifying: we emerge from it with the sense of having at last seen things as they are, of having passed from a conventional atmosphere of vaguely pious idealism to one of reality.

For, secondly, St. John of the Cross is a realist. He has no comfortable illusions, either about himself or about mankind in general. He writes as a thinker, a *letrado*, who has worked out the pronouncements which he makes on human nature; and as a skilled director of souls, fully cognizant of human weakness, putting his finger on vices that masquerade as scruples, or as virtues, and unflinchingly exposing them to the light of day. Fearlessly, if sometimes perhaps less bluntly and crudely than St. Teresa (who, strange tò say, often strikes one as the more masculine character of the two), he calls things by their proper names, refuses to excuse or parley with vice and error, rejects euphemisms, compromises and benefits of the doubt, sees and presents things as they are.

His own life, as we have already observed, will triumphantly pass the acid test of comparison with his teachings. In him we find material poverty conjoined with poverty of spirit, detachment of spirit allied to that of sense, a continual attentiveness to the voice of God coupled with a continual care for the needs of men. Anyone who supposes withdrawal from the world to be selfish, spiritual mortification unpractical or converse with God impossible has only to study a life in which are so clearly portrayed purgation, illumination, union, and the Dark Nights of the Soul—in short, the Mystic Way in its entirety.

All this, provided he can accept the Saint's postulates and share his ideals, the Christian of to-day finds in the highest degree attractive. Whatever the faults of our age, the time has gone, let us hope never to return, when among professedly Christian people calculated and consistent hypocrisy is recognized, tolerated and even admired as being artistic and clever. A man may succeed in living a double life, in professing and preaching virtue while practising vice, in deceiving his closest associates as to his ideals and conduct, but he will keep his duplicity to himself, for, once he is found out, his credit and reputation will vanish. Sincerity, consistency, outspokenness, courage are the qualities in a man which make the widest and most powerful appeal. Facing the facts, knowing the worst, seeing problems and difficult situations as they really are—these are the attitudes which we try to cultivate in ourselves and in others. These virtues, these qualities, these attitudes we find to a very high degree in St. John of the Cross.

Next, I believe that, once he understands the Saint's teaching, the genuine Christian of to-day will welcome its severity. For so long as its ideal of self-sacrifice was regarded from a Victorian easy-chair, it looked like mere barren and pointless asceticism, to a modern and enlightened civilization quite unintelligible. But now that nineteenth-century standards have gone, and we have come to a moment in history when we have to fight and struggle and suffer for things which in our simplicity we had thought of as our inalienable birthright, the life and ideals of St. John of the Cross look very different. Once we realize that the asceticism in his teaching is a means to the greatest end within the conception of man, it assumes a new light altogether. We have learned from our national experience that suffering, even to death, may often be necessary, and is always well worth while, for the sake of attaining intangible and imponderable benefits. Choosing the difficult instead of the easy, the wearisome instead of the restful, the disagreeable rather than the pleasant has to-day, in our ordinary world, become almost a commonplace. Is it, then, any wonder if the heroes of the spiritual life, who have long since learned to do this, should begin to seem more practical folk than we had ever supposed them to be? For, after all, we are making sacrifices to obtain a corruptible crown, but they are incorruptible.

What St. John of the Cross demands of us, as we have seen, is a severity with ourselves proportionate to the desirability which we attribute to the spiritual ideals after which we are striving. No reasonable man can think that demand other than reasonable. Millions would respond to it were it ever put to them as starkly and clearly as he puts it. He calls us from the hothouse atmosphere of a religion sponsored by fashionable churches or popular newspapers into the keen bracing air of the religion of the Gospels. In the unhealthy heat our spiritual energy is wilting: a sojourn on even the lower slopes of Mount Carmel will revive it.

And now we rise to a higher plane. For the mystic in St. John of the Cross, as well as the ascetic, must hold an attraction for every true Christian. It may be said of all mystics, but to our Saint, since he is among the greatest of them, the saying is especially applicable, that they have an intrinsic value for us which it is entirely beyond our ability to estimate. For, just as mediaeval explorers brought home the news that there existed lands which their fellow-countrymen had never 'seen, and probably never would see, but the existence of which they would henceforward take on trust, so the mystics, one after another, with a unanimity independent of age, creed or race, bring us reports from a country, more difficult to chart than any on earth, which, but for their testimony, might be supposed to exist only in the imagination.[4] The time has passed when intelligent Christians could reject the cumulative evidence of all the mystics, or dismiss it as of no concern to them: few thinking people can deliberately do that to-day, and even these few are sometimes overborne by the weight of evidence. No one has charted more of this spiritual land than St. John of the Cross. And, though it may never be our "happy chance" to make the journey, the knowledge that the goal exists is surely an invitation to us to tighten up our spiritual life and nerve ourselves to set out for at least a small part of the way. Nay, even the most humdrum routine of our lowly workaday lives must be illumined by the

[4] As St. Teresa puts it, in her usual matter-of-fact way: "If the Lord grants you these favours, it will be a great consolation to you to know that such things are possible; and, if you never receive any, you can still praise His great goodness. For, as it does us no harm to think of the things laid up for us in Heaven, and of the joys of the blessed, but rather makes us rejoice and strive to attain those joys ourselves, just so it will do us no harm to find that it is possible in this our exile for so great a God to commune with such malodorous worms, and to love Him for His great goodness and boundless mercy." (*Interior Castle*, I, i.)

knowledge that far above us, other souls—elect, heroic souls indeed, but "subject to like passions as we are"—are receiving supernatural graces. To know that there is a beauty greater than any we ourselves have seen or can imagine should not make us discontented with the drabness of our own lives but help us to appreciate more deeply such beauty as may be given to us either now or in the future. To know that God gives Himself on earth to those who can lay aside every weight and struggle upward till they meet Him should fill us with praise for His goodness and determination to struggle ourselves for as much of the way as we can.

At the very least, the reading of these authentic records of communion with God will quicken our spiritual sensibility. As we grow accustomed to being caught up by their irresistible force and made to breathe the pure, invigorating air of Mount Carmel, we come down in heart and mind more and more reluctantly to the plain. Who, after reading the life of St. John of the Cross as it really was, and after absorbing, not merely commentaries upon him but his own genuine doctrine, could possibly go back to conventional hagiography, to enervating accounts of lives that seem to have been a medley of supernatural "favours" and an orgy of spiritual "sweetness," or to books which try to dilute our Divine religion, to eliminate the supernatural from it and to reduce it to purely human standards? To live for a time with the interpretations of life created by

the world's greatest masters of it in literature, music
or painting is never again to find complete satisfaction in inferior company. Just so, once our taste for
spiritual things is formed on the *Ascent,* the *Dark
Night* and the *Spiritual Canticle,* our own standards
will be raised to a higher level. We shall better realize the overwhelming greatness of God and our own
incredible diminutiveness. As a result of this, we
shall seek to approach Him in His way, not in ours.
We shall become less dependent upon, and even less
tolerant of, the meretricious, the puerile, the ephem-
eral element in popular methods of devotion. Our
ideals will expand; we shall glimpse new and more
splendid horizons; our life will develop a new unity
and singleness of purpose. And all this, and more,
both because of the magnetism of All-Holiness, Who
alone has the power to draw all men unto Him, and
because the Saint, in so many words, assures us that
we can follow some part of the mystic road, if only
we will, and inspires in us hopes, however faint, that
we may do so. "And every man that hath this hope
in him purifieth himself, even as He is pure." So,
through the living and energizing activity of this
master-mystic, not only we, but those with whom we
associate, shall become, in however slight a degree,
more like to God.

Though a plain-dweller, I may travel to a land
where I shall live many thousand feet above the level
of the sea and find snow-capped peaks all around me.
At first the change may not be easy to grow accus-

tomed to, nor even pleasant; and, being no Alpinist, I may never in fact scale a single one of those peaks —only in a secondary sense will they become my familiar friends. But I shall soon become very different from the person I was in my home on the plain. From the keen air I shall draw greater physical well-being. I shall live more intensely; work harder, play harder and sleep harder. And it will be astonishing, even though I never become a mountaineer, if I do not soon find myself starting to walk up the nearest hillsides instead of being content with strolling along the valleys or the village street.

What is more, there will come a day when the valley is choked with drizzling mist and one side of the village street can hardly be seen from the other. What is it on that day that will inspire me to brave the rain and set out up the mountain path to see if I can climb above it into the sunshine? And, even if I fail, shall I not reflect that if I lived on the plain there would be no such opportunity?

So it is with the writings of a surpassingly great mystic like St. John of the Cross. We come to him knowing nothing of the Mystic Way: we find him, on the one hand, rather uncomfortably outspoken; on the other, embarrassingly enigmatic and obscure. But there is something about him which stimulates us, perhaps without our knowing it, and soon we feel the better for reading him: in fact, although we have neither ability, nor time, nor perhaps inclination, for the contemplative life, we find ourselves in several directions developing more spiritual energy and ambition. Then there comes a time when the mists of doubt or sin descend on us and St. John of the Cross tells us that so long as we sit down under them and allow them to overwhelm us we shall never escape from them. The only way out, he says, is the way up: we must climb.

> Through such souls alone
> God stooping shows sufficient of His light
> For us i' the dark to rise by.
>   *And I rise.*

Index